The GPO produced a number of propaganda posters during the war. This message, from the The Ministry of Homeland Security, highlights its role of 'listening to the enemy'. It was quite an accurate portrayal of the work that the station was involved in.

The very highest priority in personnel and material should be assigned to what may be called the Radio sphere. This demands scientists, wireless experts, and many classes of highly skilled labour and high-grade material. On the progress made much of the winning of the war and our future strategy, especially naval, depends.

Winston Churchill
Their Finest Hour, 15 October 1940

LISTENING TO THE ENEMY
War Comes to a Cornish Village
St Erth Radio Station (1939-1964)

MICHAEL GRIFFITHS

Listening to the Enemy – War Comes to a Cornish Village

© Michael Griffiths

First Edition published 2022

Frontispiece: The St Erth Radio Station operators

Design & Typeset: Tobi Carver

This updated edition printed in 2024 by:
Bretonside Copy, Plymouth
www.bretonsidecopy.com

ISBN 978-1-7398890-0-5

Listening to the Enemy
War Comes to a Cornish Village
St Erth Radio Station (1939–1964)

by

Michael Griffiths

DEDICATION

The book is dedicated to the men and women who served their country
at the Radio Security Service Station, St Erth, Cornwall,
during the Second World War.

CONTENTS

Listening to the Enemy
(.-.. .. ... - .-. .-. .-.. .--. / - --- / - .... / . -. . -- -.--)*

The German General, Heinz Guderian, with an Enigma machine in a half-track being used as a mobile command centre during the Battle of France, 1940

* Title in Morse Code

Chapter One

Where it All Began

- The Question That I Did Not Ask
- Setting the Scene
- The Station

The Question That I Did Not Ask –
(What Did My Father Do During The War?)

IN THE SPRING of 1984, Harry Griffiths sent an audio tape to the author – his youngest son. In this tape he related the story of his early life in Liverpool and family events – seemingly nothing of great import. However, there was a postscript on the tape which was not listened to at the time.

During July of 1984, Harry quite unexpectedly died. It wasn't until a number of years later that the tape was played again – including his closing comments:

> *"You see, I don't think any one of you know what duties I performed during the war years. What would you say if a little boy said to you Uncle Mike, what did your daddy do in the war? I wonder what you would say?"*

By the 1980s, the veil of secrecy that had clothed Bletchley Park was beginning to lift and its hugely important wartime role was being revealed. In that tape, Harry Griffiths was willing to reveal to his family the part that he had played in the Bletchley story, but the opportunity to ask the question that he was ready to answer had passed.

The following narrative is an attempt to answer that unasked question.

Harry Griffiths in retirement

Setting the Scene

HARRY, LIKE MANY of his generation who served during WW2, spoke very little about the duties that he undertook throughout that conflict. All we knew as a family was that he worked at the radio station at St Erth, where he used his considerable Morse skills listening to 'Gerry' in Lisbon and to a German spy ring in North America. Whilst listening to the latter, he had recognised the 'fist' of an American radio operator with whom he had been in contact, as a 'Radio Ham' before the war.

Being an enthusiastic Radio Ham, he had a cupboard jammed full of radio equipment. Secreted at the back of that cupboard in an envelope was a little black book – 'the Code Book'.

He very rarely referred to it and yet its contents held some of the most 'secret of secrets' of Bletchley Park and went some way to explain the role that the radio station at St Erth played when Western Civilisation held its breath. The book, with its pages full of radio nets of the German and Italian war machine, was written in our father's unmistakably neat hand.

Following his passing, it lay undisturbed in a drawer in my eldest brother's house. But the world was changing fast and Bletchley Park had come dramatically into the public domain. Gradually, the tremendous role that it had played during the war was becoming common knowledge and interest in the subject was gathering pace.

In about 2011, a researcher in Cornwall began looking at the role that St Erth Station played in the conflict. One thing led to another and the existence of the Code Book became known. I then became involved and made contact with the Archivist of the Radio Security Service – the MI6 wartime organisation that ran the station.

It was only then that the full import of the Code Book became apparent. But, I run ahead of myself; first I must bring Harry from his home city of Liverpool down to West Cornwall in the spring of 1939, and then the story can be told.

St Erth, 1946, photographed by 541 Sqdn RAF

A Scouser Goes West

HARRY GRIFFITHS WAS born in Liverpool in 1912. As he grew up, he developed an interest in all things radio; it was very much a cutting edge technology in its day and my family believed that he learnt Morse whilst in the Scouts. He clearly showed a natural ability and could send and read Morse at over 30 Words per Minute (wpm). A Morse word is 5 characters in length.

He applied for a Call Sign (CS) in the early 1930s: a legal requirement for amateur radio operators – and to this day such folk are still known as Hams. His CS was G2DFH. By the mid 1930s, he was employed as a Post Office Engineer in and around Liverpool.

When Hams make contact with one another they often send a card recording their transmissions. These cards are known as QSL cards - this is Harry's card.

During the late 1930s, as the gathering storm clouds of war intensified, a government minister – Lord Sandhurst, himself a Ham, was tasked to seek out those in the country who were proficient in Morse. At some point our father would have received a rather polite letter from Lord Sandhurst asking him if he would be prepared to give of his skills for King and Country.

At this time, the General Post Office (GPO) ran radio stations across the country. As an employee of the GPO, he was very quickly offered a position. The inside cover of the Code Book reveals that two locations were offered: Thurso, Caithness, in Scotland or St Erth in West Cornwall. He chose St Erth, reasoning that Scotland would be cold and wet and maybe Cornwall would be warm and wet!

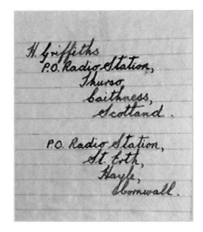

Within 18 months, he had met and married Betty Whear. Many such liaisons occurred between the men at the station and local girls.

An interesting fact was that Harry's marriage certificate showed his occupation as 'Civil Servant'. Secrecy was of paramount importance.

Harry worked as a civilian well into the war. He would have been a very familiar sight in the village going on and off duty, either cycling or by the military bus.

Registration District	PENZANCE.			
1940 : Marriage Solemnized at _Methodist Chapel._ in the District of _Penzance._ in the ___				
Columns :— 1	2	3	4	5
No. When Married.	Name and Surname.	Age.	Condition.	Rank or Profession.
35 November Twenty- Third 1940	Harry Griffiths	28 years	Bachelor	Civil Servant.
	Elizabeth Varker Whear	25 years	Spinster.	—

Left: Harry and Betty's Marriage Certificate showing Harry's occupation as 'Civil Servant'

Harry in civvies

To avoid awkward questions or brushes with the Military Police, Harry would have carried the below document.

But MI6 began to be concerned that young men, not in uniform, were attracting too much attention. It was decided that they should be enlisted into the Royal Signals at Hanslope Park.* Harry was enlisted on November 13th 1943. The deal was that at the end of hostilities he

Harry's registration at Hanslope, Nov 13th 1943

This solider has been enlisted for special duties, on termination of which he is entitled to a free discharge under K.R's para 390 XVII (c).

This man is on special duty and has permission to wear civilian clothes.

Signed P.G. Sly Lt

Lieut-Colonel

Commanding, S.C.U. No. 3.

* Hanslope Park is still a very important Government facility and is home to the technical development department of MI6 (Q in James Bond speak). In its vaults are secreted over 1.5 million documents relating to the machinations of the British Government dating back to the 1850s.(1)

could immediately return to his job with the GPO.

I have often been asked – "did Harry know who his real employer was?" Two facts would have been noted by him: firstly, as a 'top end' Morse operative he would have been very well paid – approximately £7:50 a week. (The average wage throughout the war was in the order of £4.75.) Secondly, and far more intriguingly, he was paid gross! No employee of MI6 paid tax during the war. Also his 'signing on' paperwork stated he was not paid from Army funds. This was correct as his employer was MI6 which came under the auspices of the Foreign Office. It is still so today.

Harry's 1940s Radio Station pass

A Marconi 365 Morse Key used by Radio Security Stations and other MI6 operators in WW2 and on into the post-war years

The Main Radio Station Site

IF YOU TAKE the road out of St Erth and travel up St Erth Hill, pass the Iron Age fort known as Carnabargas, continue along Steppy Down Road towards St Erth Praze, you could easily miss a dilapidated single storey concrete building on your right. It is in a field close by the edge of the road. This is the guard/generator hut of a very secret and important war time radio listening station and, together with its sister sites across the country, it had a profound effect on the outcome of World War 2.

This is the site of the Military Intelligence 6 (MI6) Radio Station, St Erth. It is one of the stations which were the 'ears' of Bletchley Park – the now famous government WW2 codebreaking establishment. It is said that the work at Bletchley Park shortened the war by at least two years. But, without such listening stations, Bletchley would have had no codes to break!

The station's guard/generator hut

Why was the station sited there? My research points to some basic facts: the high ground would help with signal transmission around the world; there was a need for sites across the full length of the UK for Direction Finding (DF) purposes; it was far away from any towns which could attract marauding enemy planes; its remoteness would also reduce the amount of prying eyes; it also had an added bonus – a water supply.

Construction started at a frantic pace in early 1939. Jimmy Hanlon* an operator at the station, told his daughter that he started work sitting on orange boxes as the tradesmen busied around him. The Intercept Field was owned by the church. The surviving documents reveal that the rent was £35 per year – with the proviso that it would be returned to its original use post hostilities. Across the road, the DF field had a different landowner; it was part of Trenedros Farm, farmed by Mr Edmund Roberts.

Fast forward to 1946, an RAF aerial photograph (shown on page 17), details the development of the site. The aerials for the station were above the Interception Hut – just out of sight. The guard hut is still in place. The well worn pathway out across the field to the DF hut is very evident.

---

* See 'The Man Who Turned The Lights Out', p88.

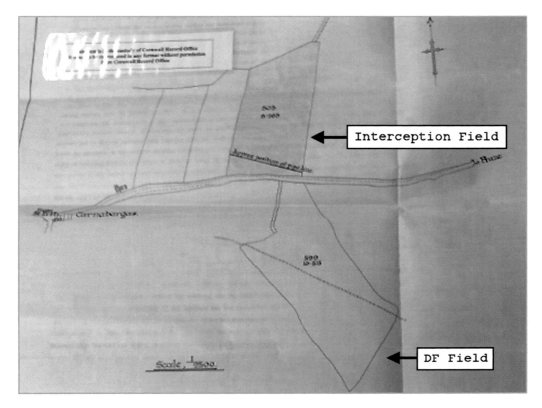

This map is dated 2nd August 1940

An RAF aerial photograph showing the station site in 1946

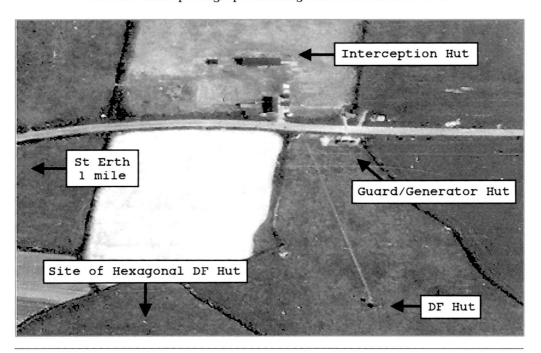

NB: Refer to 'Station Anecdotes' for more details of the site.

Initially, the stations were run by the Post Office for MI8 and every one of them had an intelligence officer on site. But, early in the war, MI6 took over responsibility and set up an umbrella organisation called the Radio Security Service (RSS). The RSS ran the stations until the end of hostilities.

Inside The Interception Hut at St Erth – at the end of hostilities

The Hughes Radio Organisation (HRO) receivers shown (above) were a superb piece of American equipment and they were used in all the interception stations. The microphone enabled the operator to speak to the 'Concentrator' – a kind of Controller seated in the same hut who was in direct contact with Arkley View.* Arkley would convey to the Concentrator where the operator should be searching across the wavebands. Each operator had two HROs, as sometimes they could listen to both ends of the wanted Axis stations when the frequencies were known.**

Over 1000 HROs were imported during WW2

* See page 25.
** For more detailed description refer to 'Stories Behind the Faces', Ken Reid – p81.

The Underground Tank at Mably Farm, Townsend

AS WELL AS the main site, there was an additional installation which was buried in a field at Mably Farm. In conversation with veterans that worked at St Erth, many did not know of this site. My eldest brother, David, vaguely remembers driving past the area with Harry who pointed to the field gate telling him that he had worked there during the war. I personally remember him saying that it was in the middle of a field and that he had to climb down into the tank, past a sten gun hanging by the ladder.

I am grateful to Barrie Smith of Townsend, who did a considerable amount of research and much of what is now known about this site is to his credit.

The idea of concealing a listening station underground is not new; avoiding aerial detection was of paramount importance. The structures used by the GPO/RSS were manufactured to a standard design based on a naval barbette (gun turret).

The Steel Barrel Cos Works constructed tank leaving the company's Uxbridge workshop

The Mably tank was manufactured by J & F Pool of Hayle and its dimensions were approximately 6m in diameter by 3m in height. This information was supplied by Mr Jack Harris of Plymouth, whose uncle worked at J & F Pool and helped to build it and fit it out.

The ground was prepared and the tank buried in approximately 1942. The power to the site came via an underground cable straight across the fields of Tregenhorne Farm, from the generator at the main radio station. One benefit to Tregenhorne Farm was that it became one of the first farms in the district to have electric lights.

A local farmer, Mr Trevor Rodda of Gear Farm, remembers the road by the guard hut being dug up and cables being laid. He said that there was a picket

---

The two photographs below show a tank, similar to the St Erth tank, that was manufactured at the Steel Barrel Cos Works, Uxbridge, during the early stage of designing and installation of such structures. They are dated 27th August 1938.

Hatch to underground chamber

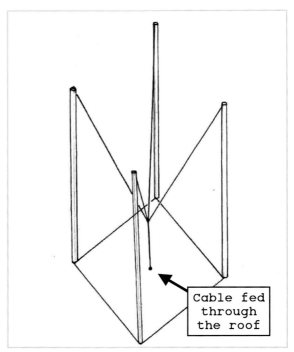

Cable fed through the roof

This is the only known picture of the site. The fourth mast is just out of the picture - on the left. The photographer would have had his/her back to the road gate. The configuration at the top of the tank clearly shows the square hatch to the underground chamber.

Barrie Smith's drawing, from Trevor's recall, of the mast configuration. Trevor's memory is very accurate!

fence running from the guard hut out across the field to the site of the tank and that there was a flourishing garden next to the guard hut. He also remembers the aerial configuration which is confirmed by the only photo that exists of the top of the tank.

I recall Harry saying that during one long night shift someone walked over the top of the tank. He was on duty on his own and it frightened the life out of him – the thought of having to perhaps use his duty sten gun made him even more petrified. He, like many of his contemporaries, disliked the military aspect of his work – being made to march around the field at the main site and learning to fire a sten gun was not something he enjoyed.

This picture shows Gerry Openshaw (CS - G2BTO) who is seen here operating in a DF tank, using a goniometer. You can just make out the tank ladder to the right of the picture. The goniometer was a device that allowed the operator to get a DF bearing on an enemy in a very short time. This picture was taken at another RSS site.[1]

The Underground DF site at Mably Farm, Townsend
Picture taken circa 1946 by 541 Squadron RAF

Over a 100 people worked at St Erth Station, around the clock, until the end of the war. Because of the shift roster, not all staff are in this picture. Many non military local people also worked at the site in ancillary roles. This picture was taken during March 1946, in front of the main Intercept Hut. Top row (left to right): Clayton, Baron, Hill, Proctor, Wright, Westren, Munson, Pragnell, Webber, Cowley, Hobman, Jack Garrack, Ernie Pace (T), Hanlon, Cpl Griffiths (DF), Robertson (DF) and Terrill. Middle row: Hobbs, Prince, Chamberlin, Alex Tough, Martin, Goodchild, Neve, Cox, Shewring, Collins, Murray, Fletcher, Ward, King (T), Percy Baverstock (Driver) and Galpin. Bottom row: Grimson, Sgt Hurn, Locket, Locket, Moore, Sgt Arthur Oakes, Cpl Tom Eyre, Capt Scarret, Lt Orr, Sgt Walters, Cpl Sandy Powell, L/Cpl Wellington, Reg A Court (T) and Sgt McLeod. Seated on the grass: Frank Barnett, Roy Snowdon, Benjamin H Cheeseman, Debble, Trevathen (T), Ken Reid, Geoff Wade and Gordon Allen (Driver)

The Bletchley Web

BEFORE WE START to delve into the chapters unravelling the Code Book, it may help the reader to have an appreciation of where St Erth Radio Station fitted into the 'web' of Bletchley Park. I am indebted to the late Geoffrey Pidgeon for his very clear pictorial overview on the following page. I have, however, adapted his graphics for the purposes of this book. Geoffrey worked at Whaddon Hall, the wartime home of MI6 (Section VIII) – the organisation of which St Erth was a part.

As can be seen, the RAF, the Army and the RN all had their Y stations across the country. They primarily listened to their enemy counterparts.*

Included in the matrix was the RSS whose prime role was to listen to the enemy's Secret Services. There would have been occasions, of military necessity, when each station would cross boundaries to add their expertise.

An example would have been when over 20 Y stations were involved in tracking the German capital ship – the *Bismarck*. St Erth certainly helped in listening to the German and Italian Navy. However, because of the nature of the role of the RSS, there would have been a very marked reluctance to ask for any assistance from the General Service.

The intercepted messages from the Y stations found their way to Bletchley Park as **Unprocessed Data**. The decoded intercepts were described as **Comprehensible Intelligence** and these priceless decoded messages were sent by teleprinters to the various organisations of the British War Machine.

Windy Ridge is at Whaddon Hall and from there, the decoded messages were conveyed to the various theatres of war by the Special Liaison Unit**. The decoded RSS intercepts were passed on to MI6 and the Double Cross Committee.

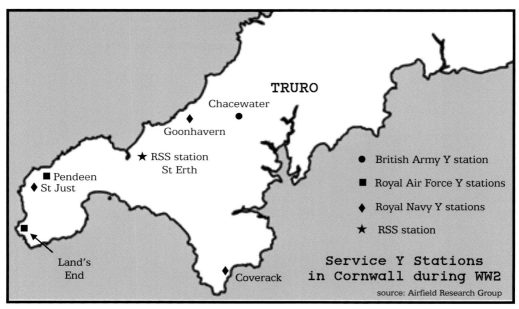

TRURO

Chacewater

Goonhavern

RSS station
St Erth

Pendeen
St Just

Land's
End

Coverack

● British Army Y station

■ Royal Air Force Y stations

◆ Royal Navy Y stations

★ RSS station

Service Y Stations
in Cornwall during WW2

source: Airfield Research Group

* Wireless Intercept became WI – pronounced Y and such stations became universally known as the Y station/Y service and so on.

**National Archives HW 49/1, HW 3/119,120.

The Web of Military Intelligence Gathering via the Y Stations

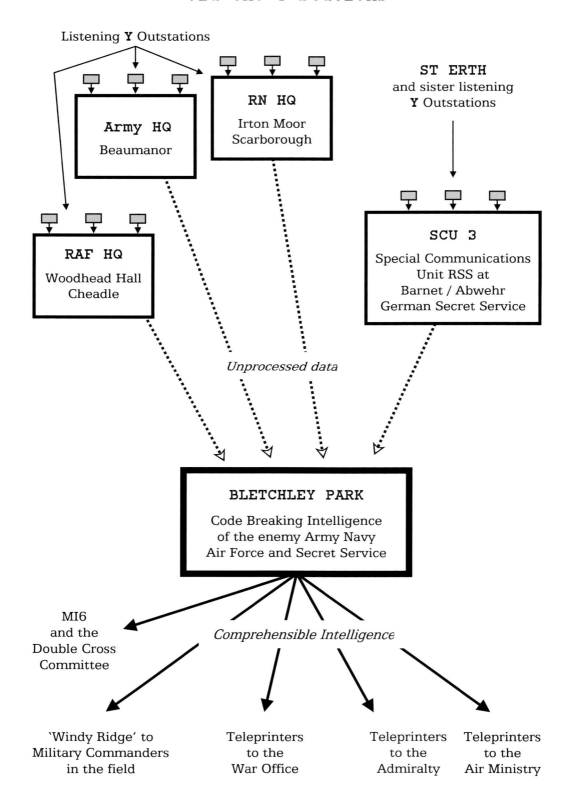

RSS Station Phonelines

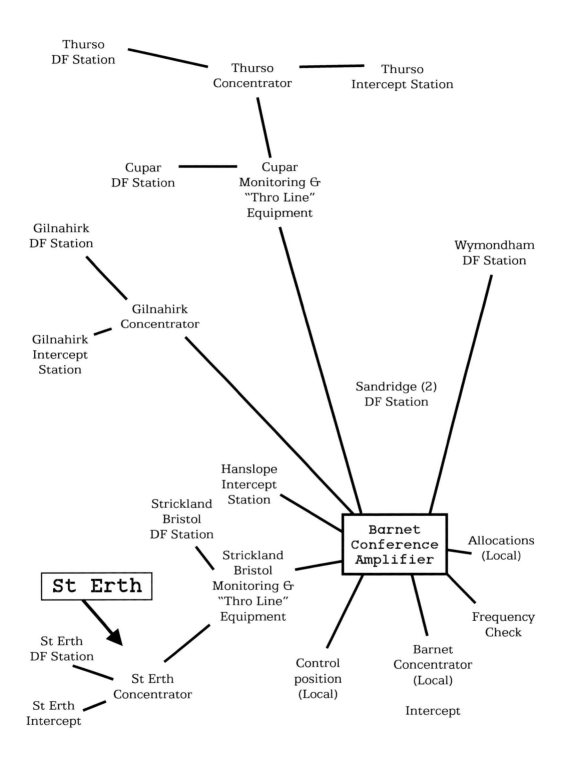

This diagram shows all the dedicated telephone line connections to RSS Stations and its principle organisation centres at Arkley, Barnet, together with HQ at Hanslope

The Headquarters of the British and German Radio Wars

The country estate of Bletchley Park was the HQ of the British Codebreakers

The country house in Wohldorf, just outside Hamburg, where the Germans listened to the British and American Radio Traffic

Chapter Two
The Code Book

The GPO set the station up in the early part of 1939. The operators were of a very high calibre and they were credited with picking up enemy transmissions across Europe. A document held in the BT Archives, London, record their achievements.

> It is of interest to note that the existence of well organised groups of enemy low power short wave stations working on the continent, was first noted by a group of Post Office operators at the Post Office/R.S.S. intereeption station at St.Erth.

The vast area that was being covered by St Erth Radio Station is clearly shown in this page from the Code Book.

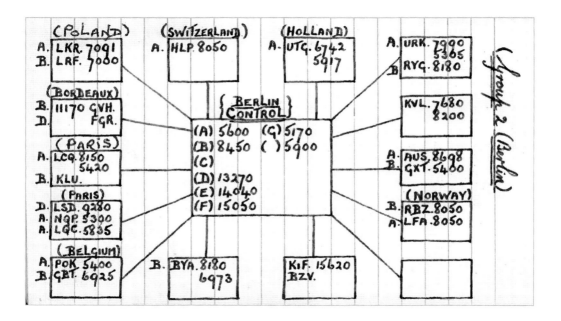

It should be noted that this net detailing enemy Call Signs - LKR, LRF, etc, and frequencies - 7091, 7000, etc, was just a moment in time. Within 24 hours both Call Signs and frequencies would all change. It is thought that A, B, C, etc, refer to different enemy operators at the same location, but I have no way of confirming this.

The Code Book — Some Background

IN ITS DAY, the Code Book encapsulated the main purpose of the RSS – to listen to the enemy's Secret Service. Principally, this would have been the 'Abwehr' – the German Secret Service. But, as will be shown, St Erth also listened to the German Navy, the Italian Navy, the German Gestapo, the Sicherheitsdienst (SD), the Russians and the Japanese and probably many other countries which we will never know about.

So by definition, the book was an immensely secret document: Ultra secret * – the security level concerning the nation's utmost secrets. All things concerning Bletchley Park were at that level. Very few people, besides Churchill himself, knew the significance of what was going on there. It is estimated that less than a 1000 people throughout the war were privy to that information - which is quite remarkable. The contents of the Book with its radio nets, International Brevity Codes and Group Numbers, would have been very familiar to the operators at the station. Without a doubt, if Harry was found off site with the book it would have been a very serious security infringement of the highest order. So why did he write it? We believe that as he worked at two sites: the main intercept station and down in the underground tank at Mably Farm, the book would have been a very useful aide-memoire. It was small enough to be secreted in his army tunic and would have been a handy reference when on duty – perhaps on his own in the middle of the night when listening to call signs and varying wavelengths.

Tracking enemy signals would have been very difficult, but an accomplished Morse listener could recognise the characteristics of the Morse sender's 'fist' – which is as clear as a signature or voice and so could be tracked wherever it turned up on the wavelengths. This, of course, would have tremendous strategic value when tracking the enemy's movements. Operators were able to say where the Morse sender had previously been heard on a frequency and, in doing so, added to Bletchley Park's ability to build up indepth wallcharts of the movement of enemy forces.

An RSS veteran, Gerry Openshaw, whilst recording his memories for the Imperial War Museum, made some interesting comments with regard to the nationality of those to whom they were listening. He said that they could recognise an Italian immediately – 'they would send their Morse in a very fast and erratic nature with many mistakes, which made it very difficult to read'. Another veteran said much the same, adding that you could almost see their shirt tails flying in the wind! Gerry said that the French operators were worst than the Italians. The Germans, however, were very precise, easy to read with hardly ever any mistakes. Was this down to training or just temperament? (1)

The book is very much a moment in time and it does not seem to have been written in any particular chronological order. The radio nets were used to give a simplistic and logical layout of the locations of the Abwehr Agents – recording the CSs and wavelengths that were used to contact Berlin. It is

---

* **Ultra** was the term adopted by British Military Intelligence in June 1941, for wartime signals intelligence, obtained by breaking high level encrypted enemy radio and teleprinter communications at the Government Code and Cypher School, (GC&CS) Bletchley Park.

Hugh Trevor Roper

thought that Hugh Trevor Roper, later Lord Darce, who was an officer with the RSS, devised this format. (2)

Hugh Trevor Roper (HTR), visited St Erth at least once during the war, staying at Carnabargas – a 10 minute walk away from the radio station. The guesthouse was run by a Mrs Taylor – her children recall her telling them that he was a quiet, retiring person. He came to West Cornwall to recuperate from a bout of Erysipelas – a very painful skin infection. He would have obviously visited the radio station during his stay; in fact his decision to stay in St Erth may well have been influenced by the proximity of the station.

HTR relates an amusing incident in his posthumously published book 'The Wartime Journals'.(3) Whilst walking through the lanes near Penzance, he was apprehended by members of the local Home Guard. They must have thought that his spectacles gave him a Teutonic look. When asked who he was and what he was doing there, he refused to tell them. This, of course, heightened their conviction that he was some kind of 5th columnist. He was then apprehended and a round of phone calls ensued. Eventually, they were ordered to release him by the authorities. He found the whole escapade very amusing. It must have been - because he was not known for his sense of humour.

A typical radio net layout that all the station's operatives would have been familiar with

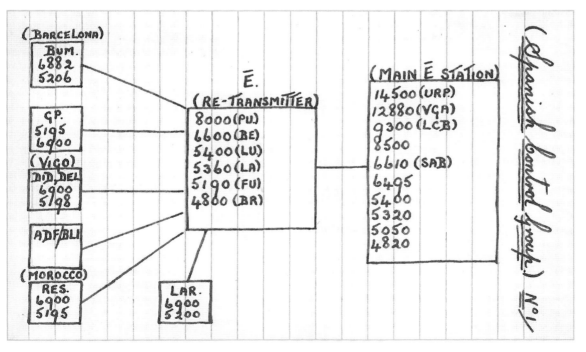

The Enigma

THE GERMAN RADIO operators would send their messages through the Enigma in a five digit format.

The Enigma Machine was an encryption device, developed and used in the early to mid 20th century, to protect commercial, diplomatic and military communication. It was employed extensively in all branches of the German military during WW2.

As used in practice, the Enigma encryption proved vulnerable to cryptanalytic attacks by Germany's adversaries – at first, Polish and French Intelligence, and later, by a massive effort mounted by the United Kingdom at Bletchley Park, as part of the Ultra program. Whilst Germany introduced a series of improvements to Enigma that hampered decryption efforts to varying degrees, they did not ultimately prevent Britain and its Allies from exploiting Enigma encoded messages; they were a major source of intelligence during the war. The Machine shown is a 3 rotor version. The configuration of these rotors was only in use for 24 hours and at midnight the configuration changed for the next day. If the code was cracked for any one day – at one minute past midnight work would have to start afresh on the new code for the new day. The German Navy (Kreigsmarine) used a 4 rota version which made decryption much more difficult and contributed to the hugely successful U boat campaign. The RSS recorded these transmissions on log sheets.

An Engima machine

The Log Sheet would have been sent to Arkley (near Bletchley), for sorting and then taken to the appropriate hut at Bletchley Park for decoding

Name H.KING					Region HN		
Address		R.S.S. Log Sheet			Group		
File No.Y/HN/353					Sub-Group OXFORD		
			BERTIE				

DATE AND TIME O.M.T.	CALL AS RECEIVED	MESSAGE AND REMARKS				FREQUENCY Kc/s	WAVE LENGTH M.	TYPE OF SIGNAL	STRENGTH
9.12.41. 1700	CZE	QSA0 PSE CALL "K "SRI QSA0 QRX NEXT QRVA			NW73	5400	CW	3
1800	E	NIL HK ND 22ND 349RM (QRM BLOTTED & OUT)				5400	CW	3
1800	GGG	QTC (LISTENED TILL 1915 BUT ND)				6200	CW	2
1915	WEB URK	QTC CT 935/71 - (VY HEAVY ATMOSPHERICS) 4880					CW	3
		AOHLC	VUBAK	"NKUZ MHPXN	LTHPK			
		XFGEL	WOFYH	RDZFZ RZAXP	DFJZB			
		TYHNN	OPLDU	NECIW FSJGS	QVYIG			
		DVDQX	WBDMJ	MHRWW NKLFW	UFF "O			
		THZGQ	OOVKW	CZEHQ MWEKE	HZ "ZM			
		IQOD MIWF VXAOU		KOVYW MESKD	ANGXX	5190	CW	2
	DUF	RPT W35 PSO QSY						
	URK			"HCT T "FX		4900		

This first page in Harry's Book shows the German Brevity Code, which was in a standard international format. It was used by all countries as shorthand when sending messages. It enabled the sender to use three letters to convey information very simply. Often, the German radio operators would send a message in code through the Enigma Machine and then use the Q codes to converse with the recipients in plain text. Their fist and location would be recorded and relayed to Bletchley Park.

German Brevity
Code

P.O. RADIO STATION
ST. ERTH
(GERMAN CODE.)

QZA. Destination
QZB. Engaged. Working DX.
QZC. Telephony. QSL on MGE.
QZD Will call you later
QZE. Freq. too high.
QZF. Freq. too Low.
QZG. Can you relay on ---- Kc/s.
QZH. Hr. Noflation
QZJ. Deciphered correctly
QZK. Call ---- to GA.
QZL. Message undecipherable.
QZN. I have not received Message
QZP. I have Transmitter trouble
QGL. Send V's or C/Sign.
QBL. Raise your Freq.
QBJ Lower your Frq.
QDY. Ans. Me Ans. Me.
QHY Received
QBN. QSY Shift Freq.

Nauen
Q Codes

Nauen 'Q' Code.
QMC No Traffic
QMB I have Traffic
QVI Closing down.
QMA. How are my Sigs
QHA. How are you receiving.
QLI. Have you any Traffic.
QMR. Message received
QIR. Send V's
QVF. Wait until ----- (4 or 5 figs.)
QPP. Transmitter Breakdown
QVB. Unable to Ans.
QVW I do not hear you
QOA. Repeat Traffic
QLA. Reply at -----
QIM Stand bi.
QJN I do not hear you.
QZG. Your note is bad.
QVR. Send V's or c/s.
QMS. Please acknowledge.

Nauen 'Q' Code.
QVM. Stop Transmission.
QLB. Your sigs are poor.
QLF Is my Freq. correct.
QDI. Commence Traffic
QOL. Repeat all.
QVE. Make Sked.
QRG. I have ----- words
QVG. When is next Sked.
QWB. Is my wave correct.
QOK. Repeat Transmission.
QLH. Send words twice.
QVZ. Undecipherable.
QJL. Raise Freq.
QZJ. You are being jammed
QZB. Unheard
QMI. I am ready.
QHO.
QDY.
QBN.

Listening to the Kreigsmarine

VERY LOW FREQUENCY radio transmission was mainly used to carry Morse signals and was used to communicate with the Kreigsmarine (the German Navy) and, in particular, the U boats. These Morse signals could penetrate to a depth of 20 meters (approx) into saltwater. The submarines could not carry the necessary transmission equipment to reply to these signals at depth so they had to almost surface to transmit; this made them very vulnerable to air attack.

Following a talk I gave to a group in West Cornwall, a lady told the story of her father who was based at an RAF Station on the North Cornish coast. He flew anti submarine sorties out in the Western Approaches. She said that as soon as a patrolling aircraft was given a bearing on a transmitting U boat, the plane would head to that location and began to circle around the position, waiting.* The U boat would then submerge, wait and surface a little way off to continue the message and when it did, the boat was attacked with devastating consequences.

The U boats sent their signals using a Kurzsignale Code System, which transmitted Enigma coded messages in very short bursts of about 20 seconds. They thought that their system was impervious to conventional DF. However, the Allies had developed a very advanced HF/DF radio detection system called a Huff Duff and it could pick up these messages and quickly give a bearing.** Up until the spring of 1943, the German Atlantic campaign was very successful, but as the British/Americans developed long range aircraft, advanced DF and weapon systems, the tide swung in the Allies' favour.(5)

Nauen, pronounced Nowen, is a town situated 38km west of Berlin. It had a Transmission Station and operated from 1906 to 1945, for Very Low Frequency (VLF) radio transmissions (traffic). Surprisingly, it survived the intense Allied bombing campaign undamaged and it operated throughout the war. (4)

The long range Consolidated B-24 Liberator, a familiar sight across the skies of Devon and Cornwall from 1943 onwards.

---

*U boat radio operators would transmit full 200 watt power for a few seconds to boil off water coating the aerial before sending the message. This produced a strange fizzing noise when intercepted and prepared the interceptors for the imminent very short transmission.

**Much of the research and development was carried out at RAF Defford in Worcestershire.

Agent ZigZag – The Three F Man

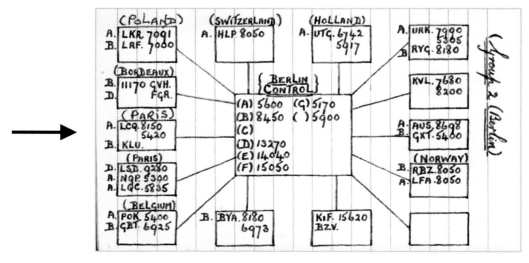

Agent ZigZag's CS in the Code Book

PREAMBLE	GROUP Nº	PREAMBLES	GROUP No's
5L/C. No Preamble.	0/40 Various.	ED NL =	0/14
5L/C. = 21/150	NAF 0/20	THIS TYPE ONE TEN =	1 & 10
175 FFF =	6/11	NOW THIS TYPE ONE TWO =	1/2
432/35 =	2	NOTE TYPE SIX HAS BBB =	6/1 6/2
XZ 35 =	2	DAGO MARY FOUR LOTS =	6/20 to 6/28
NR.21 = 1045 = 60 =	0/12	DAGO MARY AND ADD THE BBB =	6/20 to 6/28
2901 = 1730 = 20 = JYKL.	13/151 (BERT)	(Nº OF GROUPS.) =	2
FT NR5 – 10-15 0930 –	0/1	(Nº OF LETTERS.) =	1/11, 1/31, 2 & 3.
6D 17 14 1500 0 LM =	0/10	2917 85 =	7
		2917 125 =	7
		2903 125 =	0/2 & 3
		2903 125 = 2903 25	2
		2957 103 =	0/11
		1000 125 =	0/13
		2903 1630 107 251 =	1/11 & 1/31
		2903 1630 251 107	7
		10732 14325 =	} 3
		10732 14325 21703 =	} 3

FFF[6] WAS THE training CS of the famous Double Agent Eddie Chapman – Agent ZigZag. Harry and his fellow RSS operators knew him as the 'Three F Man'. Once he became a fully operational Agent his CS became FFFFF. St Erth would have been listening to the Abwehr in Paris and Chapman was sending his Morse from there.

ZigZag sent his Morse messages from Paris – which is indicated in Harry's net

MOST
S E C R E T   11 α

FFF   Fitz...

    The operator referred to as FFF is at Nantes.   There are two
parallel services from a control at Paris to Nantes, i.e. 2/375 and
2/335.   The latter service is also referred to as FFF and appears to
be used as a practice channel.

Record.   FFF was first reported on 15/7/42.
              Service 2/335 made on 20/7/42.
              On 30/7/42 it was reported that the operator FFF was ill,
              and from subsequent chat it was apparent that he suffered
              from considerable dental trouble between 30/7/42 and
              10/8/42.

Operating characteristics.

    FFF seems to be a new operator.   He is slow and makes
frequent mistakes and his formation of symbols is poor.

Characteristics of transmitter in use at present.

    Station at Nantes using call HIR on 5025 Kc/s working DAR
on 4637 Kc/s at Paris.   Times by QRX in conjunction with
Service 2/375 (see below).   The following are details of
the Nantes transmitter:-

        Frequency: Crystal-controlled.

        Note: T8.

        Signal strength in this country: Day   QSA 2 - 3
                                          Night QSA 1

Interception of Service 2/335.

    This service is very closely associated with 2/375 and comes
up just after the contacts of the latter service.

    2/375 control (Paris) uses call HQO on 4637 Kc/s and works
to OSF on 5025 Kc/s at Nantes.   Times are by QRX in DSZ.
Usual QRX times are 0530, 0800, 1300, 2030, 2230.

    On indication from control, e.g. "Pse test FFF" both
transmitters turn round and use the calls of 2/335.

J.L./
12/8/42

A Zigzag page from the National Archives file

Eddie Chapman, alias Agent ZigZag

Zigzag has no less than nine MI5 files held by the National Archives and they commenced during the summer of 1942 – so Harry's preamble list and net date from that period.

Eddie Chapman was born in Bunopfield, County Durham, and grew up in a very impoverished family. Having left school, he joined the Army and was quickly dishonourably discharged after going AWOL. Chapman very soon launched into a downward spiral of petty crime and joined a number of other criminals – using gelignite to blow up safes, they gained the notoriety of being called 'The Jelly Gang'.

After a chapter of events, during which he served time and then escaped from a Jersey jail, Chapman was arrested by the Germans who had recently invaded The Channel Islands. They took him to a Gestapo prison outside of Paris where he was interrogated by the Abwehr. Chapman convinced them that he hated the British and would like to spy for the Germans. After an extensive training period, Chapman was ready to be flown to Britain. In December 1942, he parachuted down and landed in a freshly ploughed Cambridgeshire field. He gave himself up to the local police and insisted that MI5 be contacted.

His arrival was expected; the RSS had been monitoring his Morse messages from the moment his training began by his German Controllers. He was taken to Camp 020 (The British Interrogation Centre) and after lengthy questioning, he satisfied MI5 that his desire to spy for Britain was genuine.

Some of his most notable achievements:

• By subterfuge, he saved the De Havilland aircraft factory (which manufactured Mosquitoes) and then convinced the Germans that the factory had been destroyed.

• He was asked to confirm the accuracy of the bombing of London by the V1 flying bombs. He informed the Germans that they were landing well north of London; they subsequently altered the range of the V1s and many landed well short of their target – in the Weald of Kent. Undoubtedly, thousands of lives were saved by this strategy.

The Germans awarded him the Iron Cross for his supposed excellent service, but he received no such recognition from the British. Post-war, he became a National Celebrity, but continued to live on the edge of legality. He died in 1997, at the age of 83. Why the code name Zigzag – because his loyalty was always in question.

Preambles and Group Numbers

Preambles

THERE IS MUCH more to the pages below than you would think. As has already been mentioned, the CSs would change every day at midnight. Gordon Welchman in his book *The Hut Six Story,* added observations from his time at Bletchley: *'The Morse operators could easily pick up where a new CS popped up in the net. At Midnight as the CSs changed, the German net controls contacted each outstation for acknowledgement; they would do this by using Q Codes in plain text'.*(1) This enabled the interceptors to establish the new CSs for the day. Subsequently, an operator would be able track these relatively easily and record the message.

Welchman went on to say: '*Some of our older operators were quite phenomenal, the combination of their nimbleness of thought and hearing made it possible for them to pick up signals that an automatic machine could miss'.*

The operators would fill in their RSS Log Sheet and subsequently would be advised which CS they should be listening to next. Clearly, Harry was following these particular German operators because the RSS had given him the Group Numbers to these preambles.(2)

Harry's Code Book page on Preambles

Preamble.	Group.	Preamble.	Group.
CT. 2912 1640 090 125		CT. 64	
CT. 2914 2152	7	4 4 33 figs.	1A.
CT. 2914 2152 DORUF or LAPAW =		Date. Time. No. of letters. serial.	
CT. 0809 85 or 163		CT. 4433 letters.	1B. & 10.
CT. 41046 =		4433 letters with a	6
G. de S.		5th. group of 3 similar ones.	
CT. 0703 265	Gun	CT. 35	
CT. 2112 N°216	de	CT. 432/35	
CT. Hm. Hm	Sie.	CT. XZ 35	2
CT. 2112 1605 205		CT. 2801 = 35	
CT. FT NRS 10 15	iTi.	No of letters may be	
5 fig. code or 5 letter.		preceded by XG, XZ, L or P.	
CT. 2702 0945 115 006	Mal de	CT. 167	
0707 = 5L/c	Oix.	CT. 21521 70505 073	
CT. 1D ML 5L/c.		CT. 66951 47616	3
CT. NR21 1045 60 5L/c.	Misc.	CT. 21521 70505 07344	
CT. 2150 169 5L/c		CT. 2912/1615/202	
First 2 groups same as	GP.	= STUR = 5L/c.	13
last 2 groups.			

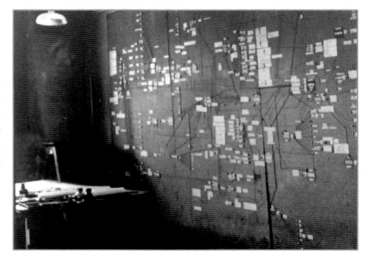

There were huge charts of German Radio Nets on the walls of Hut 6 that were continually updated as information came in from the intercept stations. (5)

In the early part of the war, Enigma encrypted messages might not be decoded for weeks or even months – certainly not quick enough to make them of any military importance. Over time, they were decoded which enabled Welchman to determine what part of the German military the message was from. Gradually his team built up very large wall charts giving details of the German military positions in the theatre of war. Welchman decided to represent the units of the Axis military with different colours. This idea was adopted throughout the war.

A preamble was the unencrypted part of a message; it consisted of the following:(3)

- The CS of the radio stations involved
  – first the sending station and then the receiving stations
- The time of the message
- The number of letters in the text
- The number of pages in the message
- The radio frequency being used
- Some information on the type of Enigma Machine being used

With each intercepted message, Welchman developed the process of examining the unencrypted part – in order to glean information from recurring patterns in this part of the communication. This process became known as **Traffic Analysis.**(4)

Group Numbers

Different German military organisations were allocated a group number and a code name. Their code name began with the same letter as the area of their controlling transmitter.(6) **Groups 1 & 6** (code name Harry), were controlled by a transmitter near Hamburg – my father had that transmitter sited at Lubeck (refer to – William Sebold, Page 47). This group was concerned with Naval Intelligence – U boats and surface vessels.

Some Notable Allied Campaigns

Spanish Control Group No 1

OPERATION TORCH (8) was the Anglo-American invasion of North Africa (8-16th November 1942). My father and his colleagues were obviously tasked to listen to the Abwehr in Morocco.(7) The region was dominated by the Vichy French, officially in collaboration with Germany, but with mixed loyalties. Reports indicated that they might support this Allied initiative. The invasion was designed to relieve pressure on their new Soviet Allies. It involved political intrigue, espionage, conspiracy and a massive disinformation campaign. It was a success for the Allies - the Germans were caught completely by surprise by the invasion.

OPERATION PEDESTAL was a British operation to carry supplies to the island of Malta in August 1942. Malta was a base from which the Royal Navy and Air Force attacked Axis convoys to Libya during the North Africa Campaign. The convoy sailed from Britain on 3rd August and passed through the Strait of Gibraltar into the Mediterranean on the night of 9th August.* Admiral Edward Neville Syfret was the convoy Commander and he was hoping that poor visibility during that night might shield his fleet's passage from German eyes. He was disappointed, however, as Abwehr watchers at Ceuta in Spanish Morocco, employed a sophisticated infrared technology to monitor all British shipping traffic. The Ceuta station was a link in the so-called Bodden Line of German Intelligence monitoring posts, built on Spanish territory on both sides of the Straits. The Bodden Line's posts were linked by radio to the Abwehr station based at the German Embassy in Madrid which had direct radio connections to Rome and to Luftwaffe headquarters on Sicily. More than 500 Merchant and Royal Navy sailors and airmen were killed and only 5 of the 14 Merchant ships reached Malta. It was, however, a strategic victory for the Allies.

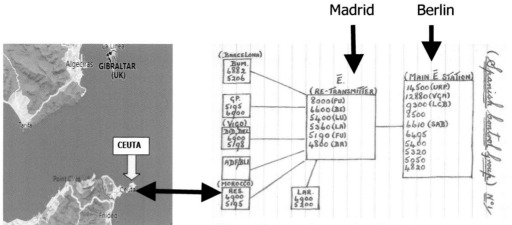

This radio net shows that St Erth was listening to the radio traffic from the Abwehr stations at Ceuta and Madrid

---

* See 'Operation Pedestal', Max Hastings, Harper Collins 2022 - page 84.

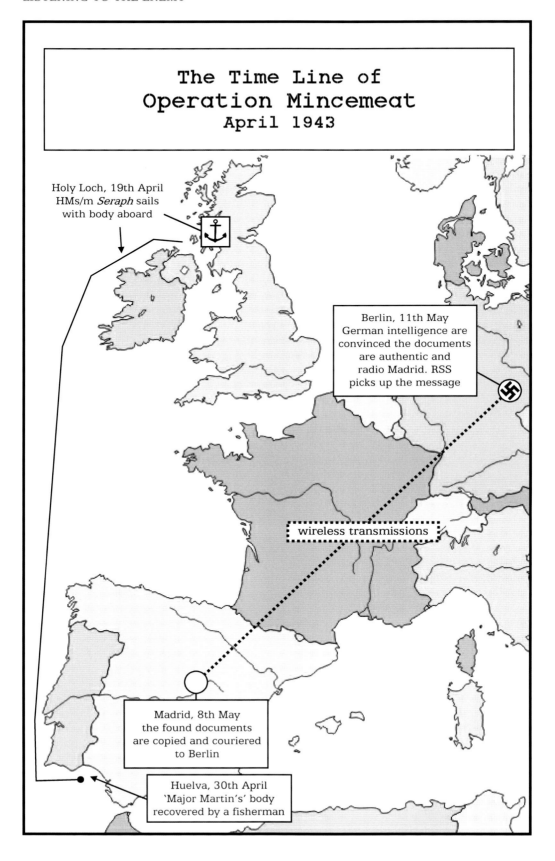

The Time Line of Operation Mincemeat
April 1943

Holy Loch, 19th April
HMs/m *Seraph* sails
with body aboard

Berlin, 11th May
German intelligence are
convinced the documents
are authentic and
radio Madrid. RSS
picks up the message

wireless transmissions

Madrid, 8th May
the found documents
are copied and couriered
to Berlin

Huelva, 30th April
'Major Martin's' body
recovered by a fisherman

Operation Mincemeat (10) took place during April 1943. A floating, decomposing body was found by a local fisherman off the coast of Huelva in Southern Spain. The paperwork found on his body identified him as Major William Martin of the Royal Marines. Chained to his wrist was a black attaché case. The contents of the case were at first given a cursory inspection by the Spanish authorities, but given their close relationship with the Germans, its contents soon found its way to the Abwehr in Madrid. Amongst the official looking documents was a letter from military authorities in London, addressed to a senior British officer in Tunisia, indicating that the Allied armies were in the throes of preparing to attack German held Greece and Sardinia. This, of course, was completely false as Sicily was the intended target. A copy of the letter was immediately conveyed to Berlin. They were totally convinced of its authenticity.

Proof that the Germans had received this false intelligence came on 14 May 1943, when a German communication was intercepted by an Ultra source of signals intelligence and decrypted at Bletchley Park. Germany had fallen for the ruse and had sent reinforcements to Greece and Sardinia before, and even during, the invasion of Sicily by the Allies. This intercepted message was more than likely to have been provided by St Erth and her sister stations. It was their task to listen to the Abwehr radio traffic between Madrid and Berlin. The previous net shows this very clearly.

A film called *The Man Who Never Was* was released in 1956. This told the story of 'Operation Mincemeat' in great detail — or in as much detail as was known about the Operation at the time. One of the support roles in the film was played by Ewen Montagu who was the same Lt Cmdr Ewen Montagu who wrote the book and was a principle architect of this hugely successful wartime operation. Despite the total cloak of secrecy over this deception plan, the Russians knew all about Operation Mincemeat (and probably before it happened!) — thanks to three of the Cambridge Five spies: Anthony Blunt, John Cairncross and Kim Philby — who headed the Iberian subsection.*

A scene from the 1956 Sumar Film Productions — *The Man Who Never Was,* depicting Lt Cmdr Ewen Montagu (played by Clifton Webb (centre) with the deception body

NB: With the continued declassification of many wartime secrets, much more is now known about this hugely successful campaign. A new film due for release in the spring of 2022 and entitled *Operation Mincemeat,* gives a far more accurate account of this deception plan.

*See The Cambridge Five — Chapter 3, Page 69.

Group 2 (Bertie) The controlling transmitter was near Berlin. This group was probably the most important one. Sub centres of the network were located in Spain, Norway, France, Italy, Poland, Switzerland, Portugal and the Balkans. All were directly linked to Berlin by daily and sometimes hourly schedules.

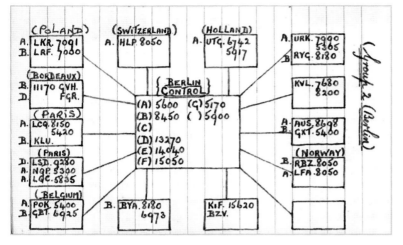

Note that the A, B, D etc in the net is a measure of the ability and accuracy of the interception

Group 2
Spanish Control Net

Although Spain was neutral during the war, it was very pro German and allowed an extensive spy network to flourish within its borders. Hitler wanted Spain to be far more involved with the war in Europe, but he found Franco, the Spanish Dictator, very difficult to handle and described his dealing with him 'like pulling teeth'.

This is another net showing the number of Abwehr Agents, their frequencies and CSs. Madrid was the most important centre for the Abwehr outside of Germany, and Berlin received regular messages around the clock from there.

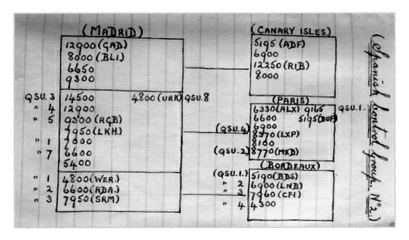

Group 2 The Fritz Sked

AS MENTIONED BEFORE, Lord Sandhurst – the Recruiting Officer, set about enlisting radio amateurs through the Radio Society of Great Britain (RSGB). Harry would have received a request to use his radio skills for the nation. However, it became quite clear that there were no illicit radio activities on mainland Britain, but the airwaves were full of enemy activity emanating from across the channel.(11)

Left Column		Group 2 Sked (FRITZ)		
C/CS. - 4475 - 1340		RUP. - 5340 Kc/s - 0600 GMT.		
ACQ. - 14050 - 1400		C/CS. - 4490 " - 0645		
C/CS. - 5990 - 1430		C/CS. - 4590 " - 0645 - C/CS. 6245		
OMA. - 6600 - 1519		MDN. - 5460 " - 0800 - FLS. 4790 " / 4280 Kc.		
RBA. - 6600 - 1549 -8000 -ARF.		? - 5115 " - 0735		
C/CS. - 6250 - 1615		RBA. - 6600 " - 0845 -ARF- 8000		
C/CS. - 6380 - 1700		C/CS. - 5880 " - 0815		
C/CS. - 4280 - 1730		BZV. - 15050 " - 0900 - 15620		
5460 - 1730		RAP. - 5400 " - 0900		
C/CS. - 8115 - 1730		C/CS. - 5375 " - 0915 - 5080 C/CS.		
NAF. - 4400 - 1800		OMA. - 6600 " - 0915 - 5579 C/CS.		
7010 - 1800		MJR. - 5400 " - 0945		
HAZ. - 5130 - 1830		C/CS. - 5390 " - 1045		
5340 - 1830		C/CS. - 4400 " - 1200		
C/CS. - 5400 - 1900		C/CS. - 6400 " - 1215 - 6900 - C/CS.		
C/CS. - 5820 - 2030		VNA. - 7950 " - 1300 - RNK - 6960		
OMA. - 4400 - 2030 - 4580, 5580, &		ARF. - 7950 " - 1300 - RBA - 6600		
6600 - 2030 - 7125 Kc/s.		AFR. - 6750 " - 1300		
C/CS. - 4400 - 2030		PSN. - 6940 " - 1300		

Lord Sandhurst sent out frequent newsletters to his staff in which he referred to the enemy as 'foxes and skunks'. One of his first circulars included descriptions of these notorious foxes - they were given names: Anna, Bruno etc. This page of skeds (schedules) refers to a fox called Fritz and he gave quite a description of this type of Abwehr transmission:

> *'FRITZ, a great fat ugly good for nothing lout struts all around six bands sowing his filthy oats all the time. Wherever you look among the kilocycles (bluebells wilt) you will find his illegitimates grinning at you. They talk all day, their fat mouths giving everybody's secrets, trying to dodge the police for they are all very much wanted.'*(12)

These intercepted transmissions were very high grade intelligence information, either between an Abwehr agent and his base, or between two Abwehr stations. Sometimes the call and reply would occur on different frequencies and employed a variety of such manoeuvres to avoid interception. By doing so, they attracted attention to themselves and aided the RSS operators. These intercepted messages were of tremendous value to Bletchley Park giving the cryptographers some of the breakthroughs they had been waiting for.

Group 2 The Norway Net — (Oslo sub-control)

OPERATION FORTITUDE WAS a deception plan in order to hide from the Germans the D-Day landings in Normandy — which took place in June 1944. After the invasion, the plan was to delay movement of German reserves to the Normandy beachheads and prevent a potentially disastrous counter-attack. Fortitude's objectives were to promote the alternative targets of Norway and the Pas-de-Calais. To achieve this there were two very well planned deceptions: **Fortitude South,**[1] to make them think that there would be an invasion across the Pas-de-Calais and **Fortitude North,**[2] to make them believe that there was to be an invasion of Norway.

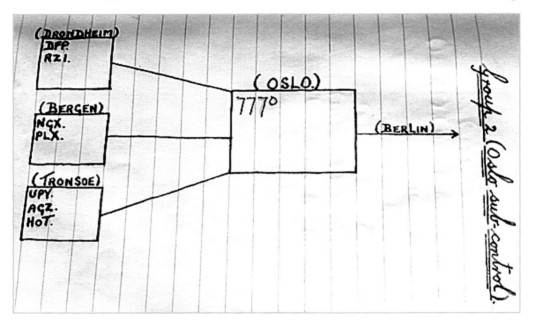

This net shows that St Erth was listening to the Abwehr activity in these four Norwegian cities and their radio traffic to Berlin. Very early in the war, in late 1939, the RSS picked up transmissions from a ship in the North Sea which appeared to be conducting the Abwehr operations in Norway. Instead of using the Enigma Machine, the Abwehr were using a hand cipher. MI5 were quite excited about this because it was very similar to a cipher used by a rising star in the Double Cross organisation — namely Agent Snow — Arthur Owens.[3] [4]

Norway was certainly of great concern to MI6 because they had two stations in Tromso (misspelt Tronsoe), three in Trondheim (misspelt Drondheim), two in Bergen and four in Oslo. Their primary objectives were to observe the main German naval movements.[5] Based in Trondheim was a secret ship watching group, code named **Scorpion,** who kept MI6 constantly informed.[6]

To add to the story, Ken Middleton, an operator at St Erth, was awarded this citation (over page) which was, according to a St Erth researcher, for his work on interception associated with Norway. Ken was an accomplished radio operator; he ran an electrical shop in Hayle post-war.

St Erth operator Ken Middleton

Listening to the *Tirpitz*

The *Tirpitz* was the second of two Bismarck class battleships. She was a formidable fighting platform. In early 1942, she sailed to Norway to act as a deterrent against an Allied invasion. *Tirpitz* was also intended to be used to intercept Allied convoys to the Soviet Union. Her presence in Norwegian waters forced the Royal Navy to retain a significant naval force in the Northern Hemisphere. The challenge of hiding this massive ship in the Norwegian Fjords was a difficult one, compounded by persistent Norwegian resistance operations. Bob Painter, a SCU3/4 veteran, recalled (in his short paper on *Direction Finding in wartime*), that each capital ship of the German Navy carried SS/Gestapo officers who would have been in regular radio contact with their counterparts on the mainland. St Erth and her sister stations would have monitored these

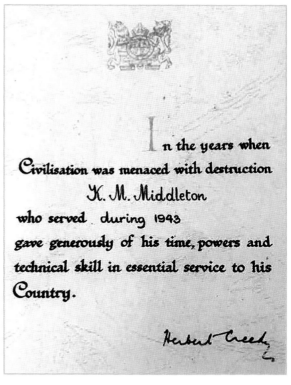

I n the years when Civilisation was menaced with destruction K. M. Middleton who served during 1943 gave generously of his time, powers and technical skill in essential service to his Country.

Herbert Creech

Ken Middleton's citation

transmissions and ultimately Bletchley Park would have decrypted this radio traffic. It would have painted a clear picture of where the vessel was and any possible future movements. The RAF, using 'Tall Boy' bombs finally sank the *Tirpitz* on the 12th of November 1944.(7) (8)

The *Tirpitz* camouflaged in the Faettenfjord – which is a side arm of the Trondheimsfjord northeast of the city of Trondheim. Trondheim appears in the Norway net, it was obviously an area of interest to the St Erth operators.

Heinrich Himmler

Groups 3 & 13 (Wille) – The controlling transmitter was near Wiesbaden. These groups were concerned with the Sicherheitsdienst (SD) – the intelligence agency of the Nazi Party under Himmler. They were closely associated with the Gestapo, with whom they eventually merged. From Bletchley Park's point of view, decrypting the SD Enigma messages was fairly easy. They were very uncouth and used four letter words often – so much so that Bletchley once deciphered a message where the SD instructed its operators to avoid using bad language in their transmissions for fear of offending female operators. From a technical point of view, they would commence their Enigma messages by using a series of four letter words – thus aiding decryption.(13)

Group 7 (Violet) – The controlling transmitter was near Vienna. The group was concerned with the Balkans, Ankara and later Greece - also the Ionian and Aegean Islands.

These pages below show the different characteristics of the British, Russian(14) and Axis radio preambles. Although Churchill ordered that the Russians were to be treated as Allies, MI6 had other ideas and they very much sanitised all the information that they shared with them. But of course, the infamous Cambridge Five spy ring was so comprehensive that all Allied secrets were conveyed to the Soviets. In fact, their leader, Kim Philby, worked for MI6 and would have known of the existence of the RSS, and the radio station at St Erth, along with all its endeavours.

Refer to 'Memories of a Signalman' – Page 81. In this account Ken Reid, a St Erth operative, relates that as soon as the war in the Pacific ended, the St Erth Station switched all its attention to the Iron Curtain countries, in earnest.

British.
If 99999 in the Text = RAF.
All call-signs include 3 letters
& mixed figures & letters.
Frequent use of ii is made
between groups.

German Naval.
1920/32 (pause) 1920/32 (pause)
6 (pause) AEXR BZRG MAKN
PQCV∧BRZG SK.
(1920 = time.)(32= serial No.)(6 = Groups
The pause is very noticeable.
Another, very definite feature is
that the first two groups are
repeated as the last two.
German Army.
Has either 2TL. 3TL. or a group
of 6 letters in the preamble.
Russian.
The letter 'R' between groups.
Italian.
Use 5 fig. cypher in which each
10th group is marked 10000.
Spanish.
Use operating sigs. P173. P231. etc

Group 10 The American Connection

HARRY SPOKE VERY little of his wartime activities, but he did talk about listening to 'a spy in North America'. This is the story of William Sebold – a Double Agent, and our father's part in this great American spy drama.

Wilhelm Georg Debroski was born in Mulheim, Germany in 1899; he served in the First World War in the German Army and, following that, left Germany in 1921. He found employment in industrial and aircraft plants in both North and South America. He became a United States citizen in February 1936, when he changed his name to William Sebold. Returning to his family in 1939, to see his ailing mother, he had a visit from the Gestapo asking him to spy for the 'Fatherland'.(1) Sebold declined, but he received another visit from the authorities; this time from the Abwehr in the guise of Dr Renken – who was actually Major N. Ritter, a Senior Abwehr Officer.

During this visit, it was made quite clear that if he did not co-operate things would not go well for either him or his family. So he agreed and was given the alias – Harry Sawyer and code name Agent Tramp. He received training, including the use of codes, Morse and micro photography. But, before leaving for home, Sebold went to the US Consulate in Cologne, informing them of these facts and of his desire to spy for America. The US Government readily agreed to employ him.

On arrival by boat in New York from Genoa on 8th February 1940, Sebold was greeted by his new employers – the FBI.(2) They helped him set up an office on 42nd Street in Manhattan. Sebold would have a cover as a Consultant Engineer. The office was bugged and had a two way mirror and a camera. Before he left Germany, Sebold was instructed to contact a prominent Abwehr Spy Chief who was in New York, called Fritz Joubert Duquesne (pronounced Doo-Cane). Following this meeting, more than thirty subagents visited Sebold's office, over a period of many months, in order to receive instructions and pass over illicit material. All of this was being recorded.

Fritz Duquesne (3)

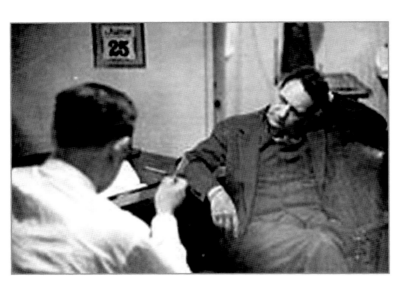

Sebold (on left) talking to Duquesne, on 42nd Street

The Radio Station at Centerport, Long Island

In May 1940, a radio transmitting station was set up, operated by FBI agents, on Long Island. A particular USN radio operator, (whose fist Harry recognised as a Radio Ham from before the war) began sending Sebold's messages to the German shortwave station at Wohldorf near Hamburg. For about 16 months, the Long Island Station sent over 300 messages and received nearly 200.(4) This is where Harry came in - having recognised the Morse fist of the FBI radio operator. He recorded this in the Group 10 net, giving details of the location of the transmission. (Harry has written LUBECK as the receiving station. Lubeck is 70km from Hamburg.)

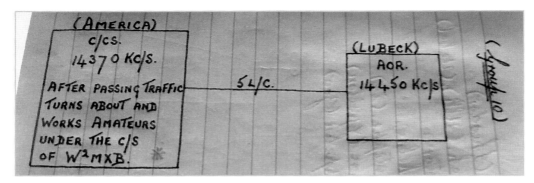

Group 10 Net

Harry's comments in the net are quite specific. After the operator sent his message, '*passing traffic*', he then begins – '*turns about*', to contact amateurs under the CS of W2MXB. In about 2014, Radio Security Service archivist Stan Ames, who is also a Radio Ham, decided to search W2MXB on the net and much to his surprise, he found that it was still active. He also found that the current user

is a Mark Henneberg and that he inherited the CS from his grandfather - a Frank Henneberg. Stan contacted Mark Henneberg and I subsequently followed this contact up and have been able to add a little bit more to the story:

During the war, Frank lived quite near to the Long Island Radio Station set up by the FBI at Centerport; he was a radio operator for the US Navy. Mark's grandmother told him that his grandfather joked about '*doing work for the government during the war*'. He would have been in his late teens or early 20s during that time. So this was the Frank Henneberg who was the Radio Ham that our father recognised from before the war.

Frank Henneberg in US Navy uniform

Once Harry had noticed this traffic, he would have passed the information along the appropriate channels. He was not the first RSS operative to have picked up these signals, but he would have been able to add his knowledge of this particular contact. Eventually, MI5 made contact with the FBI and advised them of the transmissions that their RSS operators were monitoring.

Initially, the FBI denied knowledge of any possible spying activity, but eventually they came clean and admitted that they were running a sting with William Sebold at the centre. MI5 were very keen to keep the sting going on as long as possible, but J Edgar Hoover, the Head of the FBI, wanted to bring it to a head and bask in public adulation.

Frank's QSL card

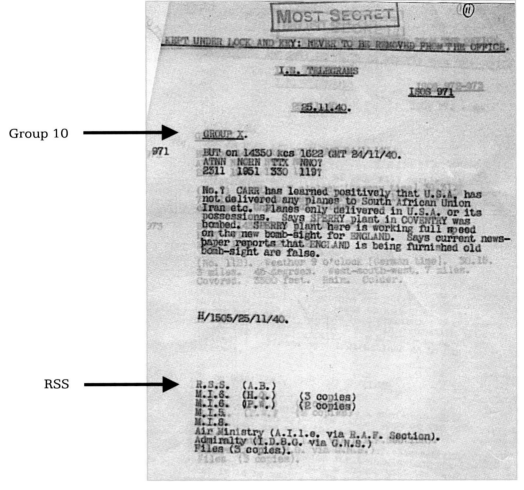

Group 10

RSS

This decrypted message could well have been picked up at St Erth; certainly the RSS received a copy from Bletchley Park

Much to MI5's disquiet, the operation was, on Hoover's instructions, brought to an end. It became known as the Duquesne Spy Ring and was the largest espionage court case in the history of the United States that ended in convictions. A total of 33 members of the German espionage network, headed by Fritz Joubert Duquesne, were convicted. On the 2nd of January 1942, this group was sentenced to serve a total of over 300 years in prison. By then America had entered the Second World War.

Movie poster for *The House on 92nd Street*

Throughout the period that the FBI ran the sting, the operatives at St Erth would have been monitoring the Morse traffic emanating from Long Island to Lubeck and back. This traffic would have been logged at Arkley View and conveyed to the relevant hut at Bletchley Park. Harry's part in recognising the first of this Radio Ham could well have played a part in identifying this FBI sting.

For wartime Britain, keeping our secrets secret was a national obsession, but not in America. This spy story was very much worthy of a Hollywood film and in 1945, a film was released which was based very loosely on the Duquesne Spy Ring and can still be seen on the internet. You will note that the street number has been altered.

After the trial, William Sebold and his wife Helen, were relocated to a new home outside San Francisco. As the years passed, he became concerned about any Nazi reprisals and he began to

Sebold and his wife Helen

suffer mentally, but he never had any regrets about his role in betraying those who wanted to do harm to his adopted country. He died in February 1970.

Frank Henneberg and his wife in the 1980s. She outlived him and passed away in January 2019. Post-war, Frank went to work at the Bell Laboratory. The family recall that he still had some association with the FBI after the war.

The Italian Subs Code

I HAVE BEEN unable to get a clear picture of the involvement of St Erth in listening to the Italian Navy (Regia Marina). Over seventy years have passed since those momentous days and I have not found anyone who can give an in-depth comment. However, these pages clearly show that St Erth was listening to the Italians. Furthermore, a local historian, Graham Hill,(1) has been researching the history of the Naval and RAF Y stations at Lands End.

```
                                    (ITALIAN SUBS. CODE.)
L.172  Anything for me.            L.034  You are being called.
L.173  5063 K6/S.                  L.036  Listen for me on ----
L.176  Anything to communicate.    L.055  Why don't you reply.
L.177  Something to communicate.   L.056  No 41 (c)
L.191  Acknowledge.                L.061  Will call you again at ---
L.206  Alter your freq slightly.   L.080  Will call you later.
L.207  No 40                       L.089  Wait.
L.208  Nothing to communicate.     L.095  Wait.
                                   L.103  No 300 (c)
                                   L.104  Repeat.
                                   L.110  Have you received No
                                   L.112  I have Traffic for you.
                                   L.113  No 300 (c)
                                   L.123  3720 Kc/s.
                                   L.128  Listen for me on Service No
                                   L.143  Yes (c)
                                   L.147  3720 Kc/s.
                                   L.166  No 360
                                   L.170  Change Freq/.
```

The Y stations at Lands End listened to the Italian Navy in the Mediterranean and to the German U Boat radio chat in the Western Atlantic. Whilst St Erth's role was primarily listening to the Abwehr, the Code Book shows that there would have been occasions, of military necessity, when their position and expertise would have been called upon for other needs. I therefore believe that St Erth's work during the war would have been very similar to that of the Lands End stations.

The Betsome Flotilla

The Italians were certainly active in the Atlantic; they ran a submarine squadron out of Bordeaux (together with the German Navy). Their submarines were known as The Betsome Flotilla.(2) They operated 32 boats, the same as the German U Boat contingent. They patrolled both in the Western Atlantic and in the Mediterranean from 1940 to 1943. They were not as efficient as their German

The ruined Submarine Pens at Bordeaux are open to the public as a cultural centre for the performing arts, exhibitions and evening events.

counterparts, but they did have some successes. St Erth was well positioned to carry out Direction Finding on their movements. The Italian Subs Codes show the radio Brevity Codes commonly used for the communication between other submarines and their land based controllers. The messages would have been sent through the Enigma Machine.

According to a St Erth operative – Gerry Openshaw, the Italian radio operators were very badly trained and as such, their Morse was very difficult to read. Whilst the Betsome submarines did have some value, it is clear why they did not meet the expectations of the Head of the German Navy – Admiral Donitz. By the 30th November 1940, Italian submarines in the Atlantic each sank an average of 200 gross tons per day. By comparison, German submarines each averaged 1,115 gross tons per day. From June 1940, three Italian submarines patrolled off the Canary Islands and Madeira, followed by three more off the Azores. When these patrols were completed, the six boats returned to their new base at Bordeaux. Their initial patrol area was the North Western Approaches and at the start they out-numbered their German Ally's submarines. Donitz was pragmatic about the Italians – seeing them as inexperienced, but useful for reconnaissance and likely to gain expertise.

The Italian submarine *Barbarigo* was assigned to the Atlantic, reaching its base in Bordeaux on the 8th September 1940, after an unsuccessful patrol. From October 1940 to May 1941, she went on three missions in Irish waters which resulted in only damaging one merchant vessel.(3)

The *Barbarigo*

Such patrols were very much in St Erth's back yard and they would have probably tracked this very submarine.

On 20th June 1943, in the Bay of Biscay, one of a pair of Whitley's operated by 10 UTU from RAF St Eval, Cornwall, was shot down while attacking a submarine believed to be the *Barbarigo*. All of the Whitley's crew were killed.(4)

The *Barbarigo*

The *Barbarigo*'s Commanding Officer was a Capitano di Corvetta Enzo Grossi who was a very charismatic submariner. In every encounter he had with an enemy ship, he would fire a salvo of torpedoes and then retire from the area claiming he had sunk it; on two occasions he alleged to have sunk a battle ship. He was awarded two Gold Medals of Military Valour and a number of promotions for his supposed acts of fearlessness. There was never any evidence of his sinkings and a post-war investigation in 1960, resulting in him being stripped of his awards.

The *Barbarigo's* Commanding Officer, Capitano di Corvetta, Enzo Grossi

The Bismarck

The Lands End Y stations were credited with establishing the first intercept of signals from the German battleship the *Bismarck*.(5) Following the sinking of HMS *Hood,* there ensued a national quest to sink the *Bismarck*. My father's diary records that he was on duty during this period and he mentioned to our sister Blanche, that he had listened to the final pursuit and demise of the *Bismarck.* He understood a degree of German and the ship's radio operators were speaking 'en clair' (plain speech); he listened to the whole drama as it unfolded. An RSS sister station at Gilnahirk in Northern Ireland, recorded its role in Direction Finding this German capital ship.(6) It was part of a country wide quest of 23 Y stations who were co-opted into listening and giving bearings on this Axis battleship. I think that St Erth would almost certainly have been involved.

The last battle of the *Bismarck* took place in the Atlantic, approximately 300nmiles west of Brest, between the 26th and 27th May 1941.

The Bismarck

Brevity Codes

('Z' Code)

ZPE. Send in plain language.	ZAP. Acknowledge please.
ZPO. Send text in plain language.	ZAN. Absolutely nothing.
ZPT. Send text in plain lingo twice.	ZCO. Send code each grp twice.
ZRO. Are you receiving me OK.	ZCS. Cease sending
ZSR. Signals are strong & readable.	ZCT. Send code each grp twice.
ZSU. Signals are unreadable.	ZCW. Are you in touch with ----
ZTA. Transmit Auto.	ZDU. We can work on Duplex.
ZTF. Transmit twice, fast.	ZFW. Auto System out of order.
ZTH. Transmit by hand.	ZFB. Your signals are Fading badly
ZTV. Transmit rapid Auto.	ZFS. Your signals are Fading Slightly
ZVP. Send V's	ZGS. Your Signals getting stronger
ZWO. Send each word once.	ZGW. Your Signals getting Weaker
ZWT. Send each word twice.	ZHC. How do you receive me
	ZHS. Send high speed Auto
	ZKQ. Let us know when you're ready
	ZLS. Disturbed by lightning.
	ZMO. Wait a moment.
	ZNN. Nothing more for you.
	ZOK. We are receiving you O.K.

('Q' Code.)

QSB. Your strength Varies.	QRA What is your name.
QSD. Your keying is bad.	QRD Where are you bound.
QSL. Acknowledge please.	QRH Does my Freq. vary.
QSO. I can communicate with ---	QRI. Is my note good.
QSU. Send on ---- Kc/s.	QRJ. I cannot receive you
QSV. Send V's.	QRK. What is the readability 1 to 5
QSY. Change to another wave.	QRL I am busy.
QSZ. Send each group twice.	QRM. Interference.
QTA. Cancel.	QRN. Atmospherics.
QTC. I have Traffic for you.	QRO. Increase power.
QTR. What is the time.	QRP. Decrease power.
	QRQ. Send faster.
	QRS. Send Slower.
	QRT. Stop sending.
	QRU. Nothing for you.
	QRV. Are you ready.
	QRX. I will call you at ----
	QRZ. Who is calling me.
	QSA. What is the strength of my sig.

BREVITY CODES ARE designed to convey complex information with a few words or letters.

Z codes are authorized for use only among military stations and they are still in use today. Post-war, they are controlled by the Combined Communications Electronics Board countries namely: Australia, New Zealand, Canada, United Kingdom and United States. These countries are, of course, also known as signatories to the Five Eyes.[*] They were close Allies during WW2, so it would appear that this Brevity code – because it appears in Harry's Code Book, was in common use.

The original Q codes were created in 1909 by the British Government, as a list of abbreviations for the use of British ships and coastal stations. Following the sinking of the Titanic, when nearby ships could not understand the sinking vessel's distress signals, there was an international agreement to adopt Q codes throughout the maritime world. The German radio operators used these codes extensively for plain speak (chit chat) before and after sending Enigma messages. Q codes are still in common use today.

Ken Reid, a St Erth operative, talks about the necessity to learn these brevity codes.[**]

U codes. I have been unable to find the solution to the U codes and so these still remain a mystery.

('U' Code.)

U 78 Have Traffic for you.
U.79 Send V's
U.88 Important Traffic for you.
U.89 Increase W/F.

U.03 Please confirm
U.05 Send V's or give receipt.
U.08 Have important Traffic.
U.12 How do you receive me.
U.15 Have nothing for you.
U.18 You are being called by ---
U.24 Have an MPA Message for you
U.26 Decrease W/F.
U.30 Repeat Message Nº ---
U.32 Have an 'O' Message for you.
U.35 Are you in touch with ---
U.39 Have a PA Message for you.
U.60 Confirmed.
U.61 How is my W/F or note.
U.69 Am having interference.
U.72 Acknowledge receipt.
U.74 Nothing for you.
U.76 Inform --- I am calling.
U.77 Have you receipt Nº ---

---

*   See GCHQ Bude, Page 100.
** See 'Some Stories Behind the Faces', Page 81.

(British Army.)
Usual Preambles NR.41, Grp 46, 54/c.
or offer of T, & Z messages.
Main means of identification
X Numbers. e.g. X279.
(R.A.F.)
Preamble similar to Army.
Call sign = 2 letters 1 fig, any
order. Figures used, 6 to 9 inclusive
(NAVY.)
Time of origin or time of receipt.
Date at end of message. X code
(German Navy.)
CT. Date. Time. No of Groups. 4 L/C.
The first two groups are always
the same as the last two groups.
(Italian.)
Preamble. Nr. Grps. 54/C. & 5 F/C.
L 159 etc. code used, also 'DA' is
used between Call signs.

This page shows that the station was monitoring and recording the unique characteristics of both friend and foe

(R.S.T.-Reporting System.)

(Readability.)
1. Unreadable.
2. Barely Readable.
3. Readable with Difficulty.
4. Readable with no Difficulty.
5. Perfectly Readable.

(Signal Strength.)
1. Faint.
2. Very Weak Signals.
3. Weak Signals.
4. Fair Signals.
5. Fairly Good Signals.
6. Good Signals.
7. Moderately Strong Signals.
8. Strong Signals.
9. Very Strong Signals.

(Tone.)
1. Very Rough Hissing Note.
2. Very Rough A.C. Note.
3. Rough, Low-pitched A.C. Note.
4. Slightly Rough A.C. Note.
5. Musically Modulated Note.
6. Modulated Note, Slight Whistl
7. Near D.C. Note. Smooth Ripple.
8. Good D.C. Note, Trace of rippl
9. Pure D.C. Note.

Add 'X' if Note appears to be
Crystal Controlled.

All messages that were intercepted would have had a RST report added to them

Phonetic alphabet is at least as old as radio communication – meeting the need for precise transmission of alpha-numeric information. During WW2 all combatant nations had standardised phonetics.

This WW2 German Phonetic Alphabet was little changed from the First World War.

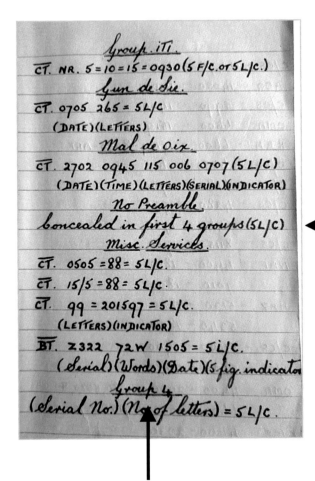

T. Toni. (Theodor)
U. Ulrich. (Ulli). (Uebel)
V. Viktor.
W. Wilhelm.
X. Xantippe. (ix)
Y. Ypern (Ypsilon)
Z. Zeppelin (Zoo)

(German Phonetic Alphabet)
A. Anton. (Anna)
B. Berger. (Bruno)
C. Cäsar. (Charlotte)
D. Dora.
E. Emil.
F. Fritz.
G. Gustav.
H. Heinz. (Hans)
I. Ida.
J. Jot. (Johann)
K. Kurfürst. (Karl)
L. Ludwig. (Luci)
M. Marie. (Max)
N. Nordpol. (Nanni)
O. Otto. (Oese)
P. Paula.
Q. Quelle. (Quatsch)
R. Richard.
S. Siegfried. (Sophie)

Group. iTi.
CT. NR. 5=10=15=0930 (5 F/C. or 5 L/C.)
Gun de Sie.
CT. 0705 265 = 5L/C
(DATE)(LETTERS)
Mal de Oix.
CT. 2702 0945 115 006 0707 (5L/C)
(DATE)(TIME)(LETTERS)(SERIAL)(INDICATOR)
No Preamble.
Concealed in first 4 groups (5L/C)
Misc. Services.
CT. 0505 = 88 = 5L/C.
CT. 15/5 = 88 = 5L/C.
CT. 99 = 201597 = 5L/C.
(LETTERS)(INDICATOR)
BT. 2322 72W 1505 = 5L/C.
(Serial)(Words)(Date)(5 fig. indicator)
Group 4
(Serial No.)(N⁰ of letters) = 5L/C.

Who or what the indicator 5L/C was remains a mystery

Group 4 was part of group 2 (see page 42) and was only active between 1941/42, this would date this page to that period

The last Net in the Code Book

THIS NET – WRITTEN in pencil and so very faint, remains a mystery. Clearly Harry felt that it was necessary to draw it out in order to make some sense of the CSs and the frequencies. It would have been in response to a request, probably by RSS Arkley View. Once received, Arkley would have categorised them and sent them on up the road to the appropriate hut at Bletchley Park for decryption. Sometimes a solution came quickly; oft times it would take days, weeks or even months.

Gradually, as the war progressed, the walls of the Bletchley Huts were peppered with nets depicting the enemy's strategies and intent. The operators in the Y stations continued to deluge Bletchley with their intercepted messages.

The RSS operators were a very accomplished group of people, but the ability of our father and his like to follow extremely faint, fast and often confused Morse,was quite phenomenal; no machine, then created, could match them. The essential contribution of these radio operators to the success of Bletchley Park cannot be over estimated. They were a prime source and without their intercepts the walls of Bletchley would have been empty and the codebreakers would have had nothing to decrypt!

It is a great travesty that, as yet, there is still no fitting epitaph to the work of the Radio Security Service at Bletchley Park.

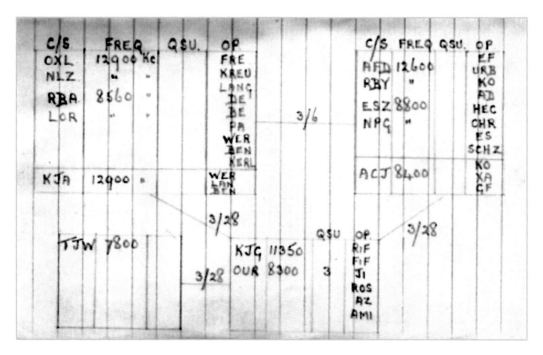

Chapter Three

The Big Picture

- The Double Cross System
- Luminaries of Bletchley Park
- The Cambridge Five
- Voluntary Interceptors (VIs)

The Double Cross System
Agents and Timeframe

Agent	Method of communication	Main Task	Date started	Date finished
Brutus	w/t	Polish affairs	Oct 42	Jan 45
Dragon Fly	w/t	Aerodromes & troop moves	Mar 41	Jan 44
Father	w/t & s/w	Air Force info	June 41	June 43
Freak	w/t	w/t re Tricycle	Dec 43	May 44
Gander	w/t	Defences in NW England	Oct 40	Nov 40
Garbo	w/t & s/w	General info	April 42	---
Jeff	w/t	Sabotage	April 41	Feb 44
Mutt	w/t	Sabotage military	April 41	Feb 44
Rover	w/t & s/w	Air raid damage	May 44	May 45
Sniper	w/t & s/w	Aircraft & anti submarine	Nov 43	May 45
Snow	w/t	General & RAF	Sep 39	Mar 41
Summer	w/t	Area around Birmingham	Sep 40	Jan 41
Tate	w/t	General info	Sep 40	May 45
Tea Pot	w/t	General	Jan 43	1945
Treasure	w/t & s/w	Projected invasion	Aug 43	Dec 44
Tricycle	w/t & s/w	General military	Dec 40	May 44
Zigzag	w/t	Sabotage, US troops	Dec 42	Nov 44

W/T = Wireless Telegraphy
S/W = Secret Ink or microphotography

The Double Cross System

MASTERMINDED BY PROFESSOR John Masterman, The Double Cross System is an amazing story of how British Intelligence penetrated and operated the German spy network within the British Isles. The British were able to identify German Agents and induce many of them to defect and supply Germany with completely false intelligence (including the D-Day deception plan). Those Agents who refused to co-operate were either imprisoned or executed.(1) To reiterate, the primary role of the station at St Erth was to listen to the 'radio traffic' of the German Secret Service (the Abwehr) who were active in managing their Agents in Britain. These Agents, of course, were Double Agents working for the British - unbeknown to their German handlers. MI5 records indicate that there were approximately 120 Double Cross Agents, but not all were on British soil and not all were of any note. In Prof Masterman's book, he has highlighted approx 39 who had an interesting story to tell. St Erth would have only listened to the Agents using W/T (Wireless Telegraphy) ie Agents using Morse Code.

The RSS monitored all of the traffic between the Double Agents and their German controllers – and the subsequent responses of the German High Command, to these messages.

I have chosen seven of the most influential of these Double Agents. Much has been written about them. The first four were pre-eminently involved in the D-Day deception plan. The remaining three were involved in general spying throughout the war.

This page from the Code Book shows the Call Signs of the controlling stations for the Agents:

Garbo was controlled by Madrid.

Treasure was controlled by Lisbon.

Tricycle was controlled by Lisbon.

Brutus was controlled by Paris.

Group 2. (Berlin)

A. Control. — 5600 KC/S.
B.   "   — 8450 "
C.   "   — (5900 KC/S)?
D.   "   — 13270 "
E.   "   — 14040 "
F.   "   — 15050 "
G.   "   — 5170 "

LFA, RBZ — WLU, NWD (OSLO)
UTG.   — (HOLLAND)
GBT, POK. — (BELGIUM)
KLU, LCQ. — (PARIS)
BID, KVL. — (BREST)
GVH.   — (BORDEAUX)
LKR.   — (LISBON)
LRF.   — (POLAND)
HRV, XUF, CXF. — (MADRID)
HLP.   — (SWITZERLAND)

Juan Pujol Garcia MBE
British codename: *Garbo*
German codename: *Alaric*

Juan was a Spaniard who visited the German Embassy in Madrid in January 1941 and volunteered to spy for them. They accepted his offer. He then approached the British at their Lisbon Embassy to offer his services. After several attempts, the British accepted and he was flown to England. Juan was able to convince the Germans that he had recruited a large network of Sub-Agents in Britain – approximately 27 of them! The truly remarkable thing was that all his Agents were fictitious – thereby, sending a high volume of disinformation. Why Garbo? – because he acted or played the part of all his sub-spies. He made a significant contribution to the success of D-Day and, arguably, became the war's most successful Double Agent.(2)

Nathalie 'Lily' Sergueiew
British codename: *Treasure*
German codename: *Tramp*

Recruited by the Abwehr in Paris in 1941, Lily subsequently travelled to Madrid and visited the British Embassy, offering to spy for them. Throughout this period, she was accompanied by her beloved dog – Babs. The British flew her to Bristol, but quarantine rules would not allow the dog to go with her. She was promised that the dog would soon follow her. Her work for the British involved sending bogus Morse messages to her German Controller concerning Operation Fortitude – the Allies deception plan. During this period, she received the news that her dog had been run over. Lily was inconsolable and as D-Day approached, she told her British Case Officer that she had been given a control signal which she could use to inform her German Controller that she was under British influence. MI5 were aghast. This news could have compromised the whole Double Cross system. Although she never forgave the British for the demise of Babs, she did not carry out this threat. She was relieved of her duties just after D-Day because it was felt that she was no longer trustworthy. However, she had made an extremely valuable contribution to the war effort.(3)

Dusko Popov OBE
British codename: *Tricycle* – German codename: *Ivan*

Dusko Popov OBE was a Yugoslavian/Serbian Playboy who was recruited by the Abwehr in 1940. The Germans believed that because he mixed with high society, including royalty, he would be of help to the Nazi cause within Britain's ruling classes. However, Popov had begun to develop, what he called – 'a little idea of my own'. He visited the British Embassy in Belgrade and offered to spy for Britain. He arrived in Bristol in December 1940 and so began a remarkable

spying career. During the summer of 1941, he was asked by his German Controller to travel to America in order to set up a German spy network and, crucially, to obtain intelligence concerning the US Naval Base at Pearl Harbour. Popov was convinced that this was to do with Japanese ill intent. He passed on this information to the FBI, but its Head – J Edgar Hoover, was not convinced and did not pass this information on to the President (Hoover took an instant dislike to Popov's loose living). In 1947, he was awarded an OBE in recognition of his role in deceiving the enemy prior to D-Day. He continued his extravagant lifestyle and died in 1981 at the age of 69 – still living the life of a young man. Why Tricycle? – it is thought that he needed two bed fellows to keep him warm at night! Ian Fleming, the creator of James Bond, worked in Naval Intelligence and would have been privy to the Double Agents. It is thought that his fictional hero was based on Popov.(4)

Roman Czerniawsk
British codename: *Brutus* – German codename: *Hubert*

Roman was a very loyal and egotistical Polish Air Force Officer who specialised in Military Intelligence. When Poland was invaded, he made his way to France. When France fell in 1940 and his compatriots left for England, he stayed and established an underground intelligence network. Following a betrayal in his organisation, Roman was arrested by the Gestapo, but he eventually convinced the Germans that he would spy for them. They accepted his offer and trained him; he then travelled to Britain and made contact with the Polish Authorities in exile. Subsequently, after much anxious debate, he was accepted into the ranks of MI5 as a Double Agent.

Roman first made radio contact with his German Controller just before Christmas 1942. He was a professional and military observer and his reports were in great detail. The Germans considered them to be of high value. However, whilst he sometimes sent his own Morse messages (under close observation), these were mainly sent by MI5 because his Morse was full of mistakes and easy to mimic. To ensure that the Germans fully trusted Roman, the MSS* revealed that the Abwehr had informed Berlin that he was a genuine source. He was used to send large quantities of disinformation regarding D-Day and in this he rivalled Agent Garbo in both quantity and quality of intelligence. The Germans' faith in Roman was re-enforced when he was tasked to send in-depth reports of the FUSAG – (First United States Army Group) – the fictitious Allied Army in Kent. Following D-Day, MSS revealed that Roman's reports were studied by Hitler and Goering.

---

* MSS: 'Most Secret Source' was the cover term used to describe the RSS intercepts and anything relating to the work of the codebreakers of Bletchley Park. This was 'Ultra Secret'.

Why Brutus? – his British Controller felt that having betrayed the Germans, he may well betray the British – as in Julius Caesar's "Et tu Brutus!". Post-war, Roman was secretly awarded an OBE for his wartime role. He settled in West London and became a Printer; married and divorced several times and kept a huge number of cats - 32! He died at the age of 75 in 1985.(5)

Arthur Owens
British codename: *Snow* – German codename: *Johnny*

Arthur Owens: Welsh Nationalist; frustrated inventor; father of a future Hollywood starlet – was an unlikely spy, yet became one of the most important

Double Agents of the Second World War. His work in marine batteries gave him access to shipyards across Europe and in the late 1930s he was contacted by the Abwehr in Germany, by Nikolaus Ritter, and asked to provide information on the capability of British Forces. On his return to Britain, Arthur contacted MI5, offering to spy for them. He was accepted and given the codename Snow.

The Germans asked him to provide identification documents for new spies being sent to Britain. When MI5 learnt of this, they realised that they had been given a remarkable opportunity to compromise every German spy that was parachuted into Britain carrying one of his IDs. This enabled MI5 to capture all the Nazi spies and recruit them into the Double Cross System.

Thanks to Snow, Professor John Masterman came to control the entire German espionage network in Britain. Why Snow? – it is a partial anagram of his surname. He ended the war in Dartmoor Prison because MI5 could not fully trust him.(6)

Wulf Schmidt
British codename: *Tate* – German codename: *Leonhardt*

Wulf Schmidt was a Danish citizen who had been recruited by the Abwehr. He was parachuted into Cambridgeshire in September 1940 under the name of Harry Williamson. He was very quickly arrested – (his arrival having been

divulged by Gosta Caroli, a previously arrested fellow German spy) and taken to Camp 020 – the British Interrogation Centre in West London. The German propaganda machine had lead its people to believe that Britain was in ruins and moral was very low. However, Wulf's journey by road from Cambridgeshire to London had clearly shown this not to be true. London was full of shoppers and traffic and undaunted by Germany's air campaign. Realising that everything he had been told was untrue, he literally changed sides there and then and co-operated fully with the British – and so commenced a very successful collaboration. On 2nd May 1945, just before the unconditional surrender of Germany, Agent Tate received a final message from his German Controller; it was full of praise and thanks for his work and particularly for his last message which related to the mining of the inlet of the Kola Peninsula. He was a most prolific and effective Double Agent – so much so that the Germans awarded him the Iron Cross 1st and 2nd class. He was involved in many deception plans, including weather reporting and military operations and was the longest serving Agent in the Double Cross System – sending more than a thousand messages throughout hostilities.

Why Tate? – because he had a very good sense of humour and it reminded his British Controllers of Harry Tate – the Music Hall comedian. Post-war, Tate became a photographer for the Watford Observer. St Erth was used to check his signal strength.(7)

Eddie Chapman
British codename: *Zigzag*
German codename: *Fritz*

For details on Eddie Chapman's life, refer to 'Agent Zigzag' – P34. (8)

The Abwehr

As the Abwehr was the RSS's principle adversary – it is worth mentioning that at its Head was Admiral Wilhelm Canaris who would have overseen all spy activities.

As the war progressed, Canaris became increasingly disillusioned with Nazism and he was implicated in a number of plots to overthrow Hitler. In April 1945, on the orders of Hitler, he was hung in Flossenbürg Concentration Camp, Bavaria.(9)

To add to the intrigue surrounding Canaris, I must make mention of Halina Szymański, the wife of Colonel Antoni Szymański, (the last pre-war Polish Military Attaché in Berlin). She was a Polish spy and also Canaris's mistress! As such, she was the Allies conduit to Canaris whilst spying for MI6. Such were the wheels within wheels that operated during the Second World War.

Wilhelm Canaris

Halina Szymański

Luminaries of Bletchley Park

BLETCHLEY PARK WAS the home of British WW2 codebreakers. A place where technological advancement and ground breaking concepts combined to lay the foundations of the Digital Age that we now live in.

During WW2, the Government Code and Cypher School (GC&CS) was based at Bletchley. By the end of hostilities its small team of cryptologists grew to well over 10,000 men and women. Their dedication and expertise made a profound and significant contribution to Allied victory. Various estimates suggest that the war was shortened by two years or more through the efforts of the codebreakers. Post-war the GC&CS became known as the Government Communication Head Quarters (GCHQ), and eventually moved to a new site at Cheltenham. There were many brilliant minds associated with Bletchley; Alan Turing is the most well know of these, but there were other individuals whose contributions deserve equal recognition; the following are just a few of those:

One could say, about the achievements of Bletchley Park, that 'in the beginning' were the Polish Cryptologists ...

Marian Adam Rejewski was a Polish mathematician and cryptologist who, unseen, reconstructed the German military Enigma Cipher Machine in 1932. In 1939, Rejewski and his colleagues – Henryk Zygalski and Jerzy Rozyki, presented their achievements to French and British Intelligence representatives in Warsaw. They had developed a hand operated multiple Enigma Machine that came up with possible solutions to German encrypted radio traffic. This creation was known as the Bomba (and it subsequently became known as the Polish Bomba). The knowledge gained from Rejewski and his colleagues enabled Bletchley Park to begin reading German Enigma messages at the start of WW2. This was seven years after Rejewski's original reconstruction of the Machine.(1) (2) & (3)

Alan Turing OBE FRS, is the most well known of the names that are associated with Bletchley Park. He is famous for being an eccentric British mathematician who conceived modern computing and played a huge part in the Allied victory over Nazi Germany. He, however, had been given a strong lead with his access to the Polish Bomba. Turing further developed the concepts and designed a machine that was immensely more powerful; it became known as the Bombe. This, in turn, was further developed in collaboration with another mathematician at Bletchley called Gordon Welchman. It became known as the Turing/Welchman Bombe. Hundreds were built by the British and the Americans during the war.(4) (5) & (6)

Gordon Welchman was a British mathematician, University Professor and author. During WW2, he was a codebreaker at Bletchley Park where he became Head of Hut 6. Bletchley was divided into huts; each hut was numbered and Hut 6 was responsible for breaking the Enigma cipher of the German Army and Air Force. Once the messages were broken, they were sent to Hut 3 for translation. In 1940, working alongside Alan Turing, he made significant improvements to Turing's Bombe, inventing the 'Diagonal Board', which greatly improved the time taken to solve the day's settings of an Enigma. Whilst at Bletchley, Welchman also spent a considerable amount of time developing a concept known as 'Traffic Analysis'. This is the process of intercepting and examining messages in order to find information from patterns in communications. It can be performed even when

the messages are encrypted. According to a BBC documentary broadcast on an American television channel in 2015, 'Traffic Analysis' was cited as the principle used in the successful hunt to locate Osama bin Laden. Welchman's work on 'Traffic Analysis' is still subject to the Official Secrets Act. He died in 1985 and never received any national recognition for his war work.[7] [8] & [9]

William Thomas 'Bill' Tutte OC FRS FRSC, was a British codebreaker and mathematician. Whilst working at Bletchley Park during WW2, he made a brilliant and fundamental advance in cryptanalysis of the Lorenz cipher; a major German cipher system. It was used for top secret communications within the German High Command. Hitler called the system his 'secrets writer'. Capitalizing on operator errors, Tutte and his team were able to understand mathematically how the Lorenz machine worked. Based on Tutte's findings, the engineers at Bletchley constructed a device which mimicked the German encryption machine. A feat, a recent BBC programme about Tutte, referred to as – 'the greatest intellectual achievement of World War 2'.[10]

Tutte's work had a huge impact on D–Day. Allied planners knew the whole German defensive structure along the northern French coast. They knew that Hitler had fallen for 'Operation Fortitude'. They also knew how many tanks and aircraft the Germans had in France and where they were based.

The late Capt Jerry Roberts, in his book 'Lorenz', said this of Bill Tutte:

'I remember Bill breaking the Lorenz system in spring 1942, whilst in the same office as him. I saw him staring

The Lorenz
Cypher Machine

into the middle distance, twiddling his pencil and making counts on reams of paper for nearly three months. I used to wonder whether he was getting anything done. My goodness he was, he had been breaking the Lorenz, without ever having seen the machine! It was painstaking work and an extraordinary feat of mind.' (11)

Bill Tutte died in 2002; he did not receive any public recognition or award for his achievements.

Tommy Flowers MBE, was an English engineer with the GPO. During WW2, Flowers designed and built Colossus, the world's first programmable electronic computer, to help solve encrypted German messages sent by the Lorenz system. He was instrumental in developing a successor – Colossus Mk2, which went into service on the 1st June 1944 and immediately produced vital information for the imminent D-Day. Flowers later described a crucial meeting with Dwight D Eisenhower and his staff on the 5th June, during which a courier entered and handed Eisenhower a note summarising a Colossus decrypt. This confirmed that Hitler wanted no additional troops moved to Normandy. He wasn't convinced that the Allies would attack in Western France. Handing the decrypt back, Eisenhower announced to his staff – 'we go tomorrow!'.

At the end of WW2, British Intelligence had access to ten Colossus machines. All but two were dismantled. The remaining two were used at GCHQ and were dismantled in the late 1950s.

In the post-war paranoia created by the Cold War, Flowers work was highly classified and he remained under the Official Secrets Act. It must have been rather galling for him when, in 1948, the Americans announced that they had developed ENIAC* – the world's first programmable computer. He had in fact done this some five years earlier, but could not disclose this. It was only in his later years that the truth came out.Tommy Flowers died in 1998.(12)

Rebuilt
Colossus Mk2

* Electronic Numerical Integrator and Computer.

The Cambridge Five

IT IS NOT my intention to reflect on the character or motives of these traitors – many books have been written about their duplicity. My research has highlighted that their traitorous deeds clearly revealed to the Russians the existence and role of stations such as St Erth. In fact, such was the volume of intelligence passed on to the Russians that they came to believe the 'Five' were Double Agents working for the British.(1) The amount of information can only be described as 'industrial'. Chapman Pincher's book *Treachery* has a chapter entitled 'Secrets by the Bagful'; it gives some idea of the sheer volume of material disclosed. I have simplified his narrative:

Traitor	Files	Contents
Philby	914	Long & detailed
Cairncross	5800	RSS/MI5/MI6
Blunt	1771	US secrets/D-Day
Burgess	4600	MI5/American secrets
Maclean	5000	Many top secret American documents

Here are some of the traitors who drew St Erth into their evil web:

Kim Philby

In the annals of espionage, one name towers above all others – that of Harold Adrian Russell (Kim) Philby. He was the ring leader of the infamous Cambridge Spies. A member of the British establishment, Philby was invited to join the Secret Intelligence Service in 1940 and began working under Guy Burgess in Section D. During 1941, he transferred to Section V under Major Cowgill and was put in charge of the Iberian sub-section, which was responsible for British Intelligence in Spain and Portugal.(2) Philby quickly rose to the head of Soviet counterintelligence and, as MI6's liaison with the CIA and the FBI, betrayed every secret of Allied operations to the Russians. He was the cause of many deaths of NATO troops in the post-war period of the Cold War.

Philby had the oversight of this net covering the Iberian Peninsula (pictured overleaf). In the early phase of the war, the GPO gave its operators a good deal of information with regard to those to whom they were listening. Harry, therefore, was able to annotate where some of these Abwehr stations were. As soon as MI6 took over, security was tightened up considerably and very little, if any, information was passed on. But, by then, operator 'fists' had become familiar, so Harry

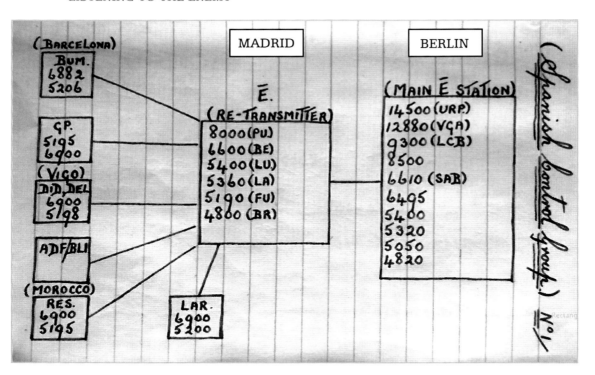

Spanish Control Net Group No 1 showing the Madrid and Berlin transmitters

and his very accomplished colleagues would have easily recognise enemy operators wherever they turned up on the airways.

Philby's autobiography *My Silent War,* mentions that by early 1942, the trickle of intercepted Abwehr traffic became a flood and that this was largely due to the work of Dilly Knox and his team who had succeeded in cracking the Abwehr Enigma code.* Little did Harry know, the information that he and his colleagues had tirelessly worked on around the clock, had been routinely and daily passed on to the Soviets by Philby. Philby mentions this in his book, saying:

> *"Every evening I left the office with a big briefcase...full of..... files taken out of the actual archives. I was to hand them to my Soviet contact."*[3]

Amongst the files of the former KGB – opened briefly during the period of President Mikhail Gorbachev's tenure in the mid 1990s, is a collection of documents that originated with Kim Philby. In Nigel West's book *The Crown Jewels,* there is a chapter entitled 'The Philby Report'; it is very in-depth and covers many aspects of MI6.[4] It mentions the RSS and all its support organisations and principal officers – in particular its Head – Brigadier Gambier-Parry. The Russians knew all about the RSS – one of the most secret organisations of the Second World War! Philby died in Moscow in 1988 – just before the collapse of the Communist ideal that he had spent his life serving. He never showed any remorse for betraying his country.

---

* Dilly Knox was a leading codebreaker at Bletchley Park.

John Cairncross

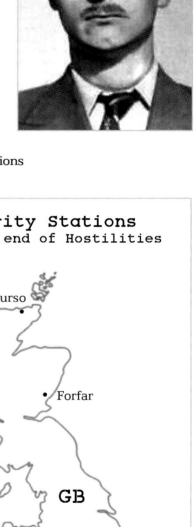

A Scottish born British Civil Servant who became an Intelligence Officer and a Double Agent. He was recruited for the Soviets by Guy Burgess in 1937 and he began working for the NKVD – later KGB. In the spring of 1939, he moved from the Foreign Office, where he shared an office with fellow spy, Donald Maclean, and after this he was transferred to the Treasury.

At the Treasury, he worked as an assistant to the head of the section dealing with the GPO and several other Government Departments. It was his knowledge of the inner workings of the GPO that enabled him to pass on the work of St Erth and her RSS sister sites to his Soviet masters. The GPO was heavily involved in the construction of a network of intercept sites around the country and in connecting them to Bletchley Park – which the NKVD codenamed KURORT. He also passed on listings of all the staff of MI5 and the locations of every one of its offices, to the Soviets.(5)

Eventually, he was moved to Hut 3 at Bletchley Park, which produced intelligence reports based on deciphered German Army and Air Force Enigma messages. He smuggled them out of Bletchley Park stuffed down his trouser legs! Subsequently, he moved to MI6 where he stayed until June 1945, and then moved back to the Treasury. Before leaving MI6, he gave the Soviets details of British Agents across Europe and South America and disclosed their plans to monitor Soviet radio relay traffic – which, of course, was St Erth's role post-war.(6)

The opened KGB files showed very clearly that Cairncross passed over two War Office Directories listing every member of the Intelligence Services. So there is a distinct possibility that every member of staff at St Erth Radio Station would have been known to the Soviets. This may explain

Radio Security Stations
from May 1941 to end of Hostilities

Thurso

Forfar

NI

Gilnahirk

GB

IRE
(Neutral)

Hanslope •
Wymondham •

Arkley

Bridgewater

St Erth

why the Soviet Radio Hams were so interested in contacting Harry as he resumed his hobby as a Radio Ham post-war; they probably already knew of him!* Carncross's status as the 'Fifth man' came into the public domain in 1979 and was confirmed by Oleg Gordievsky, the KGB defector, ten years later. He died in the South of France in 1995.(7)

Anthony Blunt

Blunt, a distant relative of the Queen and her Art Advisor, visited the Soviet Union in 1933 and was possibly recruited by Guy Burgess to the NKVD. He was invited to join MI5 after coming back from Dunkirk in May 1940. In Christopher

Andrew's *The Defence of the Realm* – page 272, he gives details of Blunt's activities. Blunt, or TONY – one of the codenames the Soviets knew him by – was involved with Philby in dealing with the intercepted Abwehr traffic. Blunt met his Soviet Case Officer, a Boris Kreshin, about once a week in various parts of London – usually between nine and ten o'clock in the evening. The Head of the British section of 'The Centre' (the Soviet name given to the department running the Cambridge Five) complained that Blunt was taking incomprehensible risks by bringing many original MI5 documents, as well as copies on film, to the meetings with his Case Officer. In Nigel West's *The Crown Jewels* – page 144, Blunt gives details of an in-depth summary of British Military Intelligence, including MI8 Wireless Intelligence – the organisation that ran St Erth Radio Station just before MI6 took over early in the war. This information was passed, via Burgess, to Moscow on November 17th 1939.

Blunt in later years

In 1963, Blunt's spying past was exposed by an American – Michael Straight, a former lover of Blunt and fellow spy. Blunt eventually gave a full confession and was granted immunity from prosecution. His confession, a closely guarded secret, was revealed publicly by Prime Minister Margaret Thatcher in 1979. He died in London in 1983.(8)

Guy Burgess and Donald Maclean

Together, Burgess (born in Plymouth) and Maclean, handed nearly 10,000 secret documents over to their Soviet minders. To what extent they knew of the activities of their fellow spies is not known. In 2016, 400 files were released by the Foreign Office and MI5. They were heavily redacted and seemed to contradict what was already known about Burgess and Maclean and raised more questions than were answered. Under the 30 year rule, much more should have been released about the pair.

The files on Philby, Blunt, Cairncross and lesser known spies such as Leo Lang and Michael Straight, have still to be made public. It is clear that the full story of the Cambridge Spies has yet to be released.(9) (10)

* See 'Harry Griffiths Post-War', Page 103.

Voluntary Interceptors (VIs) and the founding of the Radio Security Service (RSS)

MY THANKS TO the late Bob King for this short overview of the founding of the RSS.

"In the summer of 1939, Lord Sandhurst of MI8 approached Arthur Watts, who was the President of the Radio Society of Great Britain, to see if other radio amateurs could assist in a listening watch. It was thought that enemy agents or spies might be detected by short wave listeners nearby because of the strong 'ground wave' and 'clicks' produced. Radio amateurs would be ideal because they were widely distributed and, although their transmitters were impounded on the outbreak of war, their short wave receivers were not. They were given the name Voluntary Interceptors; they were in addition to the professional intercept stations that had been set up by the GPO. Very soon afterwards, these two organisations became MI8(c), but became generally known as the Radio Security Service (RSS), controlled by a Colonel Worlledge. Initially, their HQ was in Wormwood Scrubs but, because of air raids, it moved to Arkley View, not very far from Bletchley Park. Eventually, MI6 took over the RSS and it became answerable to 'C' the anonymous Head of the Secret Intelligence Service whose Communication Controller was Brigadier Gambier-Parry. Parry's organisation was growing, he already had two Special Communication Units (SCUs) designated 1 and 2, so the new Unit became SCU3. St Erth Radio Station was part of this organisation. There was also a SCU4 which was the overseas section."

Brigadier Gambier-Parry

Bob's recruitment as a VI commenced in 1941. It is worth bearing in mind that Bob was only 16 when he was recruited by the authorities! He goes on to say:

"I knew a local radio amateur – Harry Wadley G8LV, who had been a WW1 wireless operator in the Navy and he knew that I had taught myself to read Morse Code. He was already a VI, but of course I did not know that. Then things took a new and quite unforeseen course when Harry Wadley asked me if I would like to do something useful for my country. With only a vague idea of what he meant, I said yes and thought no more about it. A short while afterwards an Army Officer, named Captain Hall, introduced himself to me asking if I would be willing to give my time to some work of national importance – to which I agreed. After asking a few questions about Morse, wireless sets, the family and if I had a private room, he left with the insistence that I discuss his visit with no one outside the family. A few days

A Log Sheet dated December 1941, that had been returned to Bob

later, the local bobby called to check up on my nationality and who else lived in the house. As he had known the family for many years this was a bit of a farce.

"Captain Hall called again and I was sworn to secrecy and signed that I had read and understood the Official Secrets Act. He explained that I would be given some Morse signals to listen for and a band of frequencies on which to search for a certain type of transmission. The results were to be written on log sheets, labelled RSS, which he provided. These were to be placed inside an envelope addressed to Box 25 Barnet Herts; this was then to be placed inside another envelope addressed to the same Box 25. Sheets of stamps were provided.

"My own homemade receivers lacked stability and calibration so Harry Wadley loaned me an Eddystone All World Two, which was a primitive 2 valve set and also lacked calibration. Sometimes, I would visit him to carry out my watch on his Skyrider (a professional Hallicrafter superhet). However, I managed to purchase a Sky Buddy which, although the cheapest of the Hallicrafter range, it enabled me to do a lot of listening and therefore increased the volume of messages that I could send to Box 25. I made a regenerative pre-selector for the Sky Buddy which, although tricky to tune, made a tremendous difference to the selectivity and sensitivity.

"The signals were all weak, but from the style of sending, I got to know which would be returned stamped: 'More Please' or 'Unwanted Hun' or 'Watch Please' etc, little thinking that one day I would be wielding these same rubber stamps! It was to be many years after the war before any of us VIs were to learn that we had been listening to the German Secret Intelligence Services of the Abwehr and to Gestapo networks. All we knew at the time was that these messages were of vital importance to the war effort. Because of the low power used, the Germans did not suspect that we could hear them.

"In fact, we only discovered them by accident whilst looking for largely non-existent spies, supposedly working from Britain. There were a few, but all were soon caught and either despatched or made use of. I also recall listening to the famous Churchill speeches on the faithful Skybuddy.

"Then in January the fateful letter, which was to change my whole future, arrived from Box 25 saying, in effect, that as I would soon be of call-up age and my services could be used in the RSS. I could be enlisted in the Royal Corps of Signals (later called the Royal Signals) and avoid the normal call-up. Conditions of service and pay were included. The latter was in three bands – dependent on a Morse speed test. After some debate, as I still had my eye on the more glamorous RAF, it was decided that I should accept. I was duly sent instructions on how to find Arkley View, a house north of Barnet."

At the age 16, Bob was 'enlisted' into an organisation that dealt with the most secret of the nation's secrets. He, along with hundreds of other VIs of all ages and all professions up and down the land, together with the military Y stations, became part of the ears of Bletchley Park. Without them, the outcome of WW2 would have been considerably different and yet, nothing of what they did came into public arena until the 1980s.

Bob spoke about his work as a VI at the 2015 RSS Reunion at Bletchley Park and told the story that, many years after the war had ended, he had asked his cousin – did she know what he was doing closeted in a room at the family business each evening? Her reply was that she 'didn't have a clue'!

Bob describes this picture taken during the war: "The whole gear was housed in a massive roll top desk and locked up for security. The Sky Buddy is central and my pre-selector is above. The clock at the very top still runs! On the left is the home made practice oscillator and the Browns SG phones are on the bench. The phones were standard in RSS, but I had to buy mine".

Fast forwarding to the 21st century, here we see the late Bob King in his Shack with his war time equipment, which was still in working order

It is hard to believe that, as I write – in the 21st century, at the time when there are so many intrusive social media organisations and both friend and foe trying to get us to divulge all our personal details, the work of Bletchley Park and, in particular the RSS, had remained in obscurity until the 1980s. This is quite remarkable!

Bob organised the annual RSS Reunion at Bletchley Park. After nearly 70 years, a Commemorative Plaque was unveiled to remember the work of the VIs at Bletchley Park.

Bob seated (far right) with fellow RSS veterans at the 2013 RSS Reunion

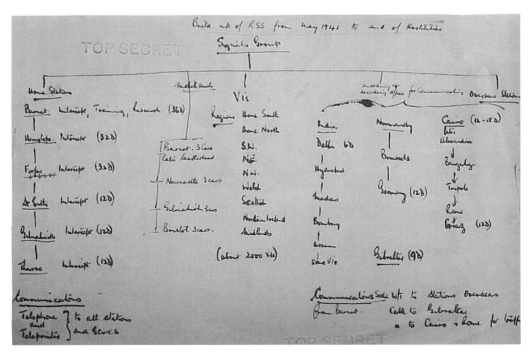

This family tree shows just how far the RSS had grown into a worldwide Listening Organisation at the end of hostilities

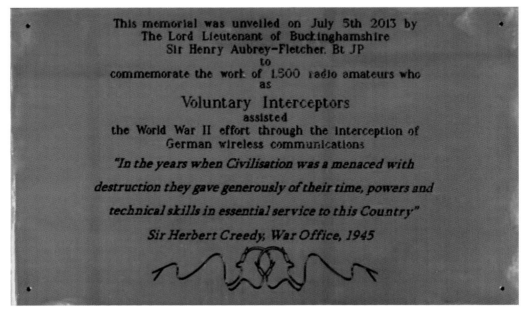

The Voluntary Interceptors' Commemorative Plaque at Bletchley Park

Chapter Four

Station Anecdotes

- Stories Behind the Faces
- The Main Site
- Mably Farm Site
- No Secrets in a Cornish Village

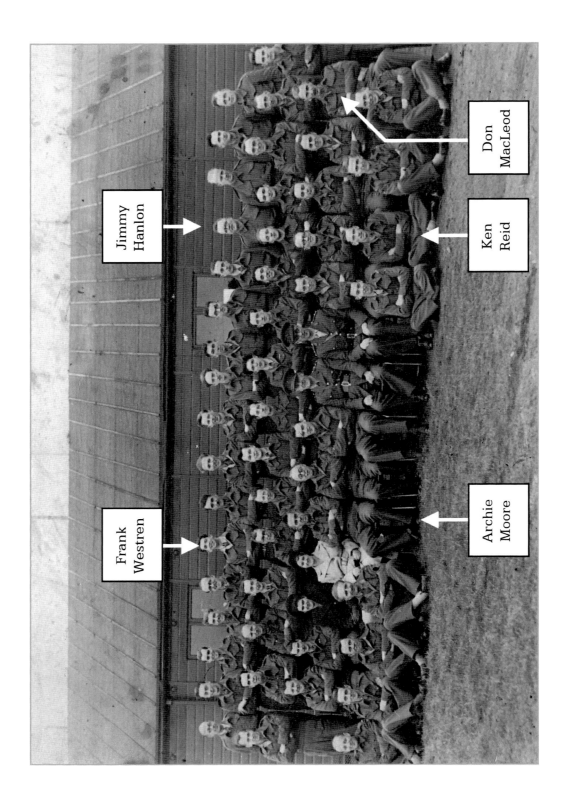

Some Stories Behind the Faces

I HAD THE good fortune to have been able to make contact with the families of a number of the operators in this picture. Each account tells a story of their time at the station and some of their life experiences.

Ken Reid
Memories of a Signalman at St Erth Radio Station

I am indebted to Susanne Hutton for this abridged version of her late father's memories of enlistment and his posting to St Erth.

"Ken Reid, like many of his generation, had learnt Morse in the Boy Scouts and had undertaken the necessary qualifications to join the Merchant Navy as a wireless operator, but was told that he was under age. Still keen to join the war, shortly after that disappointment, he was invited to an interview at the Foreign Office and, being successful, he was offered an appointment. So started his work for MI6. He was initially posted to Arkley on the outskirts of Barnet, Herts, which was only known by its postal address of PO Box 25; he arrived there in February 1944.

"At Arkley, his Morse speed was increased to 18-25 wpm. He was taught how to identify German transmissions and all manner of necessary procedures. Whilst there, he became 18 years of age and was duly issued with a uniform onto which he proudly sewed his Royal Signals flash. By the end of the course, he had reached the necessary level of proficiency and was posted to a Special Communications Unit (SCU 3) – disappointingly, not to an exotic place, but to St Erth in West Cornwall."

Signalman Ken Reid

Ken takes up his story...

"Active service was a vastly different world; listening to the enemy over the airways with atmospherics, electric storms and the Appleton Layer, played havoc with signals. There were now both ends of a link to cope with, having to keep track of both way transmissions, rapid changes of transmitter power level and rapid changes of frequency. Each interceptor had two HRO (Hughes Radio Organisation) wireless receivers. The left hand set - headset and message pad, was for transmissions received and the right hand set - was for the recipient's response. Each end of the link was operated on a different frequency and used a different call sign - always of three letters, which change frequently. The code produced by the German Enigmas was transmitted in groups of five letters.

"Interception covered the Abwehr, Sicherheitdienst, German, Italian and Japanese Embassies. There were three shifts: morning was 0800 to 1500hrs; afternoon was 1500 to 2300hrs and night was 2300 to 0800hrs. It was customary for each operator to be allocated to a specific Group transmission and so gain knowledge of the operating procedure and the 'fists' of the operators. Initially, one doubled with an experienced operator. Generally, the transmissions were to a set schedule and were monitored 24 hours a day. Between scheduled transmissions, the frequency bands would be searched for any suspect transmissions. From time to time, we would come across transmissions at 50 wpm but, although they could be read, it was impossible to write at that speed.

"D-Day was hectic and, as expected, wireless traffic increased tremendously thereafter. Also, around that time, the Germans changed their entire schedule times, call signs and frequencies, but not their transmitters or operators. Within three weeks, they had all been recovered due to the recognition of individual operators and transmitter characteristics. After D-Day, the camp guards left, presumably to rejoin their regiments, from then on the station was unguarded.

"The German operators were not rigorous with their procedures and often, after they had finished their official transmission, would lapse in to 'Ham Chat' – the international form of communication used by Radio Hams eg – VY73 means 'kind regards'. Plain language was never in German, but was more often in Spanish, which we usually managed to translate. As St Erth was listening primarily to the Iberian Peninsula, the Abwehr operators would possibly have been Spanish. As a result, dossiers of the operators, their families, where they lived etc, but more importantly – their regiments and so forth, were compiled. We were once involved in Direction Finding a transmission that was continually on the move. After a period of time plotting the various locations on a map, it was realised that they were following a railway line. It was Air Marshal Herman Goering's mobile Headquarters. All intercepts were sent by landline teleprinters, via Arkley to Bletchley Park, for de-coding.

"After VE Day we switched to monitoring Japanese traffic. Our task was to support the intercept effort of the war in the East. At the end of the Pacific War, attention was again switched and some of us were tasked with monitoring Russian transmissions."

Off Duty

"On arrival in Penzance, I was billeted in a local house and we were stuffed in like sardines. One bedroom stretched right across the upstairs front of the house and there were no gaps between the beds. As they were being paid 21 shillings per person per week, the landlords were not doing too badly.

"We mostly spent our off duty time playing snooker or darts in the YMCA, where we were able to get cups of tea and an occasional bun or some biscuits. The local Army Girls also frequented it and, as they were not paid very much, we would treat them and sometimes take them to the pictures. We also travelled further afield to St Ives, taking the Land Army Girls with us and we loved our visits to Perranporth. When the Americans arrived, the white soldiers were billeted at one end of the town and the black soldiers at the other. Girls were off limits as far as we were concerned - who would want to go out with us when they could be whisked off in a Jeep by a American who was loaded with dollars? One day I was walking through a narrow street in Penzance, going on duty, when I got caught up in an all American fight! It was unusual because they normally fought the Inniskillings (an Irish regiment) who were billeted in the town; their war task was manning the coastal guns. I was lucky to get out of the skirmish with only a broken tooth which, after a three mile walk to a dentistry caravan, was subsequently pulled out by a dentist; no injection and no gas! Things all changed after the Americans had left for France sometime after D-Day. Suddenly, we became popular again and so it was back to taking the Land Army Girls out. After a bout of sickness, I visited the MO and after a thorough examination was diagnosed with a ruptured appendix. My subsequent operation was at the West Cornwall Hospital followed by convalescence at Trewidden, a country house lent for such use by the Bolitho family.

"I recall one night – when we were tasked to do the regular clean and inspection of the station's weaponry (mostly Lee Enfields and a few Tommy Guns) that one lad was a bit premature – he had not checked the magazine and pulled a Lee Enfield trigger. Luckily, it was pointing at the ceiling and the bullet went through the roof, as did our sergeant – Arthur Oakes! We all thought it was hilarious – the guns were never normally loaded; the ammunition was kept in a locked hut some yards away."

V E Day – 8th of May 1945

"I was on duty the night before VE Day and on arrival back at my billet in Penzance, my two buddies had got their bikes out and were intending to ride over to Falmouth – nearly 30 miles away. I decided to join them; we were stopped and given free beer all the way to Falmouth! As we passed through Helston, we stopped at the YMCA for a cuppa and, hearing music, we looked out to see children dressed in white, followed by men in top hats and tails and ladies in white dresses with red bands around their waists, all dancing along. It was the annual Helston Floral Dance.

"We had supper in Falmouth and then made our way back to Penzance, just in time for me to catch the coach back to go on duty. On V E night, with very little wireless traffic, we picked up a crate of beer on the way to the station and tuned in to AFN (the American Forces Radio Network) turned up the volume and listened to the station all night.

Ken Reid and Jack Garret on route to Falmouth, stopping for some more refreshments

Ken Reid and Chas Finch by Falmouth Harbour

"When I was intercepting Russian traffic, I devised a way of establishing the frequency at both ends of a transmission. My initiative was noted and resulted in me being transferred back to Arkley for research duties – where I spent the rest of my time until demobilisation."

**Signalman Reid KJ
2603039**

* * *

Archie Moore - The *Titanic*, a Brush with Fate

Derek Moore writes:

"My father, Archie Moore, was born in 1888 and became one of the earliest 'Hams', building his own wireless equipment and erecting an aerial system in Folkestone. He told me that people used to gather outside to see his expected tightrope walking display when attaching the wires!

Archie Moore

"He joined the Marconi Company in 1908 as a wireless operator, serving on the transatlantic liners – the *Virginia* and the *Oceanic*. When the *Titanic* was commissioned, he was transferred to her as Chief Wireless Operator. However, before *Titanic* sailed on her maiden voyage, he was very disappointed when he was sent to Folkestone to assist in the erection of a wireless mast on the harbour, otherwise, you would not be reading this story! But hang on there is a twist to this tale…"

Derek Moore goes onto say that his family's links to the *Titanic* go further. "Mr Charles Lightholler, the only Bridge Officer to survive the disaster, was a great friend of my father's, having served with him on the *Oceanic*. Also Mr Cyril Evans was the Wireless Operator on the SS *Californian* when the *Titanic* struck the iceberg, though he was off duty at the time.* He was later a colleague of my brother Donovan, when both worked at the Somerton Receiving Station. Father spent some time on the liners until my mother reckoned he was having too good a time.

* The SS *Californian* was a steamship best known for the controversy surrounding her proximity to the *Titanic* at the time of the sinking. A re-examination of the facts in 1992, concerning the inactivity of the SS *Californian* in the rescue attempt, seemed to suggest the ship couldn't have added much to the saving of lives.

The *Titanic*

Charles Lightholler

"In 1913, Archie was posted to Poldhu and, after the merger of the cable companies and Marconi, became Officer-in-Charge of the Charterhouse Street branch. He then left Cable & Wireless, (C&W) and became a Morse Instructor in the RAF until joining the Royal Signals and being posted to St Erth Radio Station, where he stayed until the end of hostilities. Post-war, he returned to C&W and was employed at Electra House - the HQ of C&W. On retirement, he returned to Cornwall where he died in February 1958.

SS *Californian*

"Now here is the twist to the tale: C&W was nationalised in 1947, and all its property in the UK, except that at Porthcurno, was taken over by the General Post Office. A great clear out of records took place at Electra House and they were dumped at the rear entrance for scrapping. My father looked through the pile and came across the wireless logbook for the SS *Californian* for the time she was hove-to near the *Titanic*. We had this log at home for many years, but I have no idea what has happened to it."

Don MacLeod - A Near Death Experience!

I am grateful to Rod who has passed on this memory of his father:

"Don hailed from The Isle of Skye and attended Radio School, where he learnt Morse and having successfully passed, he joined the Merchant Navy in the 1930s. He sailed around much of the world during that period and on his last ship - The SS *Essnah*, and whilst sailing through the Mediterranean, he realised that the world was moving towards conflict and he witnessed the Italian Navy – sabre rattling. As war approached, Don left the Merchant Navy and joined the Post Office. He was initially posted to a radio station at Cupar in Fife, in October 1938, which was a sister station to St Erth. In January 1940, he was transferred to St Erth where he stayed for the duration of the conflict and like a number of GPO employees, he was enlisted

Don MacLeod with wife Hazel

into the Royal Signals (in his case not until May 1943). He spent a good deal of the war in civvies."

Rod continues: "Dad was doing a nightshift alone in the DF hut at the main station site and he was sitting at the radio - headphones on, listening for traffic - when he heard movement outside the hut which gradually got louder and eventually came from underneath the hut. Fearing that there was possibly a German beneath him, he reached out for his 303 rifle only to grasp the electric fire! It being perfectly earthed through the metal band on his headphones, it took several attempts to shake off the fire. He claimed that this was the closest he came to death during the war! To add insult to injury, the German paratrooper turned out to be a sheep looking for shelter from the West Penwith rain!

"At the end of the war, Don returned to his job with the Post Office as a Radio Engineer. True to his generation, he spoke very little about his wartime role. When the work at Bletchley Park came into the public domain, Don confirmed that he had intercepted enemy traffic which was sent on to Bletchley. He also mentioned that he visited Bletchley from time to time. Whilst at the radio station, Don met Hazel Boyns from Penzance and they eventually married post-war."

A Local Girl Remembers...
Postscript to Sergeant MacLeod's Story

A 16 year old Sylvia with Monty

Sylvia Rule nee Goldsworthy, a distant relation to the author (everyone born in West Cornwall is related in some way!) recalls meeting Sergeant MacLeod in 1945/6.

She writes:

"There were dances in the village church rooms every Saturday to raise money for the boys' homecoming fund. Mum and dad went so I went too. It must have been in 1946 that I remember Sgt. MacLeod, he was very tall and I was a little skinny shrimp – he would ask me to dance, and I only came up to about his middle! It embarrassed me that a man had asked me to dance, so every time I saw him come in I used to hide behind my friends, but he always found me – I think that he enjoyed my discomfort. He was a nice man though – but liked to tease! No one talked about the radio station. I believed that the Band was from the Army camp on Griggs Hill. They were a good Band and always let me have a go on the drums when they had their cup of tea."

Frank Westren - "I'm in the picture!"

The author wrote an article in the West Cornwall newspaper *The Cornishman* in October 2013. It included a photograph of the station staff together with a short discription of St Erth Radio Station's role in the war. A few days after it was published, he received a phone call from a Frank Westren and his opening remarks were - "I'm in the picture" – and indeed he was! Frank was quick to point out that the date of the picture was incorrect; I had dated it March 1945 and Frank said "no! it was March 1946, because I didn't join the station until September 1945". Frank told me that he was trained at Colwyn Bay Wireless College in December 1944, and after qualifying, was waiting for a shipping berth. But he then decided to volunteer for either a post at Government Communication, Bletchley Park or as a radio operator; he chose the latter and arrived at St Erth in September 1945.

He remembered my father and told me some of his own superficial memories of the station and just said that he 'listened to everything'. When I pressed him for detail, he looked at me, smiled, wagged his finger and shook his head. He was from a generation that, when they had signed the Official Secrets Act, they abided by it for life. When I left him, we both had a tear in our eye: he, having recalled those long ago years and I, conscious that I had talked to someone who had touched the world of my father.

Continuing the tradition of station operatives marrying local girls, Frank married Marie Dale. The couple were married on the 3rd August 1946.

Very shortly after their wedding, Frank (right) was posted to Sidi Bish, Egypt, with SCU4 - listening to the Israelis. Sidi Bish was known as a holiday camp for the Forces!

Jimmy Hanlon - 'The Man Who Turned the Lights Out'

Margaret Woolcock (nee Hanlon) writes:

"My father James Hanlon, known to all as Jimmy, was born in Uddingston, Lanarkshire, Scotland on 27 October 1907, and spent his formative years in Coatbridge.

Jimmy Hanlon

"A childhood accident, playing football with his brothers, unfortunately caused an injury which was to determine the rest of his life. The football had hit him on his right temple. There didn't seem to be much damage at the time, but he reported that some three days later it was as if a penny had fallen into his right eye. The retina had become partially detached. Despite the best attempts of his parents and the medical services of the time, there was no apparent remedy.

"When the time came for the choice of a career, the realm of the then nascent Radio Communications was a foregone conclusion. This love of radio was to stay with him throughout his life. Following training in Glasgow, dad joined his first ship on the Clyde in 1928, as radio operator on vessels of the Marconi and P&O lines. His log book records the various voyages over the next 11 years. He left the sea in August 1939, on recruitment to a small radio station in Thurso, where he was accompanied by my mother Sarah, also a Scot from near Largs on the Clyde coast.

"After only a few months in Thurso, there was an opportunity of a posting when various radio stations were being installed around the UK. We did not know which other stations were available because dad just told us he was drawn by the sound of St Erth; he had often joined ship at Falmouth and liked the area. We never heard what my mother thought of this choice!

"They arrived in St Erth in August 1940, and welcomed my arrival in December 1940. It is perhaps of interest that my birth certificate records his profession as an Engineer, Radio Section, GPO. However daunted my mother may have been at leaving her home and family in Scotland, she clearly came to love Cornwall and I later gained two brothers and a sister.

"Dad never told us anything of what he did at the radio station. He was very amused when he learned later that Mother Philomena, the Headmistress of St Mary's RC Primary School, Penzance, which we all attended, had altered his entry on the enrolment form which he must have filled in when we joined the school. She, assuming he had made a mistake, changed his entry from Radio Engineer to Railway Engineer! He felt this neatly avoided any questions he might have found difficult to field. Thereafter, he was often asked questions related to the GWR!

"As we grew older, our interest in what he did must have grown. In the absence of any detail from him, I think we came to the conclusion that he must have been single-handedly responsible for Hitler laying down his arms! What an achievement for a man who spent most of the duration of the war in Cornwall. Though - what would have happened had things gone otherwise and Von Ribbentrop had seen his wish granted to be appointed the Governor of the South West and resident on St Michael's Mount?!

"Up until the closure of the station in 1964, it was manned around the clock. My father spent many hours working his shift out in the DF hut in the middle of the field. From time to time, I would cycle from our home bringing his lunch and would walk out across the field and step up into the hut, which was crammed with radio equipment. Dad stayed at the station until it closed and he was then transferred to the RN Listening Station at Goonhavern near Perranporth.

St Erth DF Hut

"By this time, we were all near leaving school and going on to further education. His sight difficulties had meant that in earlier years he rode a bicycle to and from the radio station. When I was nearly 17, Dad had invested in a family car – an Austin A 55, turquoise in colour. He marshalled all his friends to teach me, and later my brothers and sister, to drive and we ferried him around. Clearly, we knew where and what the station was, but that was about all. He didn't tell us much about the dismantling of the site and he spent his last three years working for GCHQ at Goonhavern and had to be ferried there too.

"He was very pleased in December 1967, to be presented with the Imperial Service Medal by Sir Leonard Hooper at Culmhead Station in Taunton.

"What a father he was to us all. A man of great integrity, a sharp intellect, with a very good sense of humour, who despite his visual impairment, read the classics to us, spared no effort in teaching us life's skills - he and our mother giving us such a happy childhood in times that cannot have been easy.

"All of these attributes in a quiet, modest, unassuming man who inspired such love and respect. He left us in July 1982, taking with him the secrets of the immensely important task he and his colleagues did from 1940 to 1967."

He was the last operator at the station and so – *The last man to turn the lights out!*

The Main Station Site

Captain Reardon's shift, St Erth, 1943 (above)

St Erth, 1944 (above). Standing (left to right): Ron Garton, Eddie Price, Harry Rigg, Ralph Tomkins, Reg Wherry, Danny Nobbs, Joe Chamberlin, Bill Smith, Stan Groves, Geordie Turner and Reg A'Court. (Seated): Chas Finch, Ben Cheeseman, Brian Ranner, unknown, Budden, Ted Howarth and Ernie Pace

Pictured right – John McCafferty, unknown, Brian Ranner and Land Girl May. West Cornwall – 1946

Rear: Don MacLeod, Jimmy Hanlon, unknown, Harry Griffiths, unknown and unknown. Front: unknown, Jack Andrews (and Buster his dog), Capt. Varney and unknown

Top row: Sgt Moore, unknown, unknown and Sgt Oaks. Bottom row (right), Sgt MacLeod, others unknown

Don MacLeod and Harry Griffiths (centre left and right) with two unknown companions

Harry Lockett by the gate to the guard/generator hut and information board

Author's Note: This picture was taken 'post-war' judging by the information board on the hedge. I vaguely remember the board – so it would have been taken in the spring of the early 1950s. Although now over grown with blackthorn, the daffodils can still be seen flowering on the hedge early in the year. Harry Lockett was the general factotum at the station; from buying pasties to paying in cheques at the bank in Hayle, he was indispensable. Harry's daughter, Mary Curnow, nee Lockett, remembers visiting the site with her father. (See 'No Secrets in a Cornish Village' - Page 97)

(Above left) The DF Hut in the middle of the field was manned around the clock. I remember my father saying that on quiet nights he would listen to the wildlife on the prowl out in the fields. The smaller hut to its left had a very important function! Above (right) The modified DF Hut post-war, still in use in 2016. It was used for 'crib' by farm workers for many years.

Pictured above, in 2016, is the guard/generator hut in the DF field

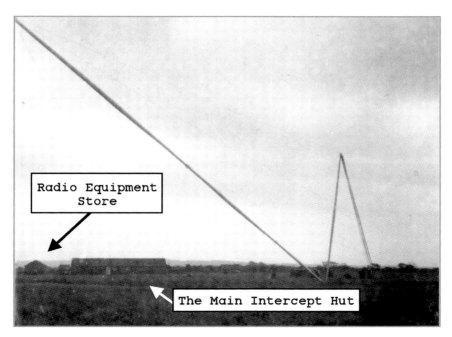

Aerials being removed post war

Shirley Thompson very kindly provided me with this photo (probably of the radio equipment store) which was still on site at St Erth in 1950. (It was then flat packed and taken to her home farm in Hayle and was still in use up until 1990.) Her father had the tenancy of this field in St Erth and was told that it was riddled with copper cables ... but he never came across any when cultivating the land! The field itself is still known as the Wireless Field. The picture shows Shirley's sister and dog Mick at the wartime hut.

Hexagonal DF Hut

An additional hexagonal shaped hut was built in the DF field but, because of the high mineral loads in the ground associated with old mine workings, this site proved to be ineffective for DF work. Originally it would have had an 'H' shaped aerial on its roof that could be turned by the operators in the hut.

This picture (below left) shows a sister site at Thurso. These huts were known as splinter-proof or shingle huts. The walls were thick, double-skinned and supposedly bullet proof.

The St Erth hut was dismantled and moved to 'Esmeralda', a large house a short distance from the station and it began a new life as a turkey coup. It remained as such until the 1970s (below right).

Aerial view of the site

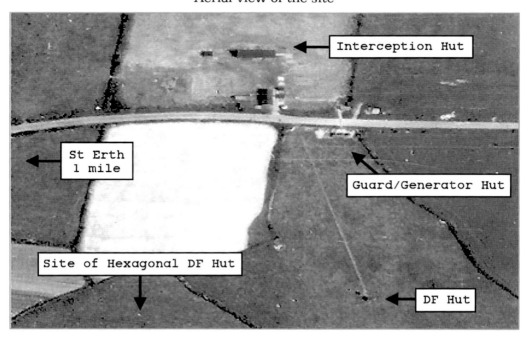

Mably Farm Site

LEONARD GREEN'S FATHER, George, worked at Mably Farm and he remembers, as a young boy, going down into the tank on a number of occasions with his father and observing an operator with headphones on. Mr Green senior had a radio receiver and wartime spares were very hard to come by. Such spares were plentiful for the operators in the tank, but fresh veg was in short supply – so a deal was struck.

Leonard recalls accompanying his father out across the field and knocking on the sliding hatch in the roof of the tank. When it opened, a bag of potatoes/broccolis was handed down and the mended radio passed back up. He also recalls that his father became quite friendly with the guards and operators.

I emphasize this familiarity because these sites were supposed to be at the highest level of secrecy and certainly no civilian should have been able to enter the tank. Yet clearly, local people were privy to, and had a good understanding of why the installation was there.

Mably was farmed by Mr Walter Honess and his two sons, Albert and Nigel. As school boys, they remember the tank being placed in the field; they remember the guards and also the garden that was planted around the guard hut.

In the 1960s, this guard hut, which was situated at the entrance to the field, was dismantled and re-erected at Rosevidney Farm near Penzance. It began a new life as a bunching and packing shed for freshly cut flowers.

Leonard Green, by the Wireless field entrance, leaning against one of the two remaining concrete gate posts from WW2. The stonework used as a footpath across the field to the tank is still in a pile in the corner of the field

Below: Mably Farm's tennant, Walter Honess, with his Chrysanthemums

Mr Honess senior was the tenant who farmed Mably from 1941 until the 1960s and he then moved back to Rosevidney. Sometime in the early 1960s, he was allowed to remove the underground tank. The structure was made from very thick steel plate and had to be cut up on site to enable it to be taken from the field.

The owner, Mr Michael Mash, then resumed the running of his farm and when I spoke to him in 2016, he recalled Mr Honess telling him that the field where the tank was situated was known as the 'Wireless Field' – and it still is. So the age old tradition of naming fields after memorable events continues. Those long ago days, when life seemed so perilous, will be forever remembered in this quiet corner of Cornwall.

During the early period of the war, the staff at the station were a mixture of civilian and uniformed personnel and displine was very relaxed. Stemming from a conversation with a Mr Mitchell, who was a station operative during the war, Sinclair McKay relates a humourous incident in his book *The Secret Listeners*, (page 139).

"A number of off duty staff from the station, whilst having a drink in a local pub, bumped into a group of regular Royal Signals who did not work at the station. This pub may have been the Smugglars Arms at St Erth Praze – which is a short walk from the station. The regulars started asking some probing questions about the station, but the station staff gave vague answers. This resulted in the regulars reporting the incident, claiming they met a group of spies masquerading in army uniform! This led to Army Command investigating the affair – resulting in a drill sergeant being sent to Cornwall to discover more. On arrival, he quickly decided to give the station staff a good dose of PT, but when he saw the state of the mature platoon all lined up, he was aghast and decided to substitue this for a walk instead. Even so, several of the men collapsed and had to be revived with cups of tea from local householders, who were heard to say 'poor old men – what dreadful treatment'."

No Secrets in a Cornish Village

DESPITE THE CLOAK of secrecy surrounding the station during the war, it was clear from the following that it was all in vain locally.

During the course of my research, I spoke to a number of people who lived in and around St Erth and also to those who attended my talks in the village. The narratives below are a summation of what was known about these two very secret sites in St Erth – at that time ...

... that the shift cycle at the station was 0800-1500hrs, 1500-2300hrs and 2300-0800hrs. Because of the remoteness of the two sites, official transport was a necessity. In conversation, one lady remembered clearly that the villagers set their clocks and daily lives on the arrival and departure of the station buses.

Mary Curnow neé Lockett in the 1940s

Talking to the late Mary Curnow, I asked her if she knew what was going on at the station. She replied immediately: 'We all knew they were listening to Gerry'. She also recalled that she would often accompany her father – Harry Lockett, who was the general factotum at the main site, and she frequently sat in the DF Hut talking to Jimmy Counter and other operators saying in her wonderfully Cornish way – 'having a bit of chat'.

The local farmers were allowed to grow corn and hay around the masts and buildings. A farmer's son, who attended one of my talks, related his father's memory of grazing his pigs around the site and that his father also remembered the mast types and configurations well.

Mary's father Harry Lockett

A good number of the station operatives married local girls, as Harry did, and football and cricket matches between the locals and station staff were regular events; it would be hard to say that they didn't know about the station and its function.

The St Erth Home Guard took turns in guarding the two sites, together with regular soldiers from the West Yorks, the Devonshire Regiment, an Irish Regiment (the Inniskillings) and the Military Police (Blue Caps).

The account of the underground tank at Mably Farm gives clear evidence that folk were aware of the installation and its equipment!

St Erth's 15th century church which stands close to the bridge that spans the river Hayle.

As the war drew to a close, the village resumed its peaceful life – its people coming to terms with the fact that there would be those who would never return.

The six inhabitants of St Erth who gave their lives in WW2			
BOND	Stewart	UK	Able Seaman
CARTER	Joseph Samuel	UK	Chief Stoker
CARTER	Samuel	UK	Corporal
LASHBROOK	Arthur Franklin	UK	Private
SMART	Stanley George	UK	Petty Officer Stoker
STONE	Melvin Pearce	UK	Trooper

Source: Cornwall Family History Society

The War Memorial in the grounds of the church – paying tribute to the dead of both WW1 and WW2 – Source: Roll-of-Honour.com

St Erth itself sustained very little war damage in WW2 although, as we now know, it played a major role throughout the conflict.

Chapter Five

Post-War

- GCHQ Bude
- St Erth at the End of Hostilities
- Harry Griffiths — Post-War
- St Erth Role of Honour

GCHQ Bude

GCHQ Bude

GCHQ CLOSED ST ERTH Radio Station at sometime in 1964, but the world was changing and wartime Allies were now becoming potential adversaries; the 'Cold War' had commenced in earnest. This necessitated the need for far larger and more technologically advanced listening sites and again, geographically, Cornwall was in pole position. GCHQ Bude, also known as GCHQ Composite Signals Organisation Station, Morwenstow, was opened in 1974. It was built on the old wartime airfield of RAF Cleave. Fundamentally, Bude carries out the same role as St Erth did throughout WW2, but with some very important differences; the much talked about 'Special Relationship' with the United States that came into being in WW2, is very evident at GCHQ Bude.

This Anglo-American site is run jointly with the National Security Agency (NSA) and GCHQ. NSA pays for most of the infrastructure and technology and GCHQ provides the land, running costs and staff. The installation is a main gateway of information into the UK and is an integral part of the 'Five Eyes' group of countries.

The Five Eyes	
Country	Membership
Australia	1956
Canada	1948
New Zealand	1956
United Kingdom	1946
United States	1946

The Five Eyes group of countries are parties to the multilateral UKUSA Agreement: a treaty for joint co-operation in Signals Intelligence. In spite of controversy over its methods, the Five Eyes relationship remains one of the most comprehensively known espionage alliances in history. There is also a Nine Eyes and a Fourteen Eyes.

At the End of Hostilities

WITH THE OFFICIAL end of the European war on the 8th of May 1945, and the war with Japan on the 2nd September 1945, the frantic days of listening to our enemies had passed and the staffing levels at the station were reducing – or so you would think. Here is a reminder of the group photo of the staff at the station and the date of the picture tells a different story. Their work was far from over as a new adversary had arisen – well not really – Russia had always been a force to be reckoned with! Churchill made a number of telling comments about the Russians. He defined them as *'a riddle, wrapped in a mystery, inside an enigma'.*

As the war with Germany developed and Russia became our ally, he quoted from Shakespeare's *The Tempest* – *'War makes strange bedfellows'.*

As has already been mentioned, St Erth was in a very important geographical position for taking DF bearings and it was involved in listening to Russia and its satellite countries as they expanded the *Iron Curtain* across Europe.* *'Iron Curtain'* was a quote from a speech which Churchill made on the 5th of March 1946 – just at the time when the above picture was taken.

Gradually, throughout the late 1940s and into the 1950s, the station staff reduced significantly as post-war Britain readjusted its defence requirements. St Erth Radio Station ceased operations in 1964.

The Ministry were true to their word with regard to Harry's release back to Civvy Street. His Discharge Certificate states: *'His services being no longer required for the purpose for which he enlisted'. Dated 9th December 1946.*

Serial No 6761

DISCHARGE CERTIFICATE.

(If this CERTIFICATE is lost no duplicate can be obtained.)

Army Form B108J

Army Number. 2602893.

SURNAME GRIFFITHS

CHRISTIAN NAMES Harry.

Effective Date of Discharge 25th January 1947.

Corps from which Discharged R. SIGNALS.

Service with the Colours : Years Three Days 74

Service on Class W(T) Reserve : Years — Days —

Total Service : Years Three Days 74

Rank on Discharge WS/Corporal

Cause of Discharge KR 1940 Para 390 (XVIII)(a)

"His services being no longer required for the purpose for which he enlisted"

Campaigns and Service Abroad

Medals

Military Conduct Exemplary.

Signature and Rank R. SIGNALS
Officer i/c Records.

Date 5 DEC 1946 19 Place READING

9 DEC 1946
ROYAL CORPS of SIGNALS
READING.

P.T.O

---

* This is confirmed by an account written by Ken Reid. See 'Some Stories Behind the Faces', Page 81.

Harry Griffiths Post-War

HARRY WAS DISCHARGED and, on the 25th January 1947, he returned to his pre-war employers – the GPO, installing telephones in homes in West Cornwall. But MI6 had not finished with him - his Morse skills were greatly needed and he was headhunted by the Ministry of Civil Aviation as a radio operator. He began working at the secret listening station at RAF Pendeen near Penzance in West Cornwall; the Cold War was gathering apace.

In 1957, he moved to 19 Group Coastal Command at RAF Mount Batten, Plymouth, and worked the RAF Shackletons that were shadowing the Russian spy trawlers in the Western Approaches.

He was instrumental in saving the lives of a Shackleton's crew when their plane, low on fuel, lost its gyros in the mid Atlantic; he was the only one on duty who could hear their very faint Mayday calls. He talked them home to their base at RAF St Mawgan. Subsequently, the whole crew came to thank him at his work place.

An Avro Shackleton from 42 Squadron based at RAF St Eval, stalking a Russian trawler off the Cornish coast, November 1956

He took up his Ham Radio hobby again and helped found the Saltash Amateur Radio Club where he taught Morse for many years.

RAF Pendeen

The shortwave bands across the globe once again began to reverberate with the much more peaceful intent of listening to old and new friends. Here is a page from Harry's Radio Log of December 1946. The pattern of contacts was similar for a number of years. Europe was a rich source of Radio Hams, probably because of the many men who had learnt Morse during the war years. What is noticeable is the scattering of Iron Curtain contacts, perhaps with a much more sinister intent!

Harry's Radio Log from December 1946, showing a scattering of Iron Curtain contacts – highlighted here with stars

Harry's Radio Log from September 1970, showing Soviet radio operators

If we move on into the 1970s, we notice a very different log page; Harry had acquired many more local Radio Ham contacts associated with his Radio Club. He mentioned to the family that he would often be pursued by Iron Curtain Hams keen to make contact and wanting to know more about him.* He was still working as a radio operator for the Ministry of Defence and, therefore, he was of interest to the Russians. British Naval Intelligence would, from time to time, visit our home to inspect his Amateur Radio Station Log, which he meticulously kept up to date.

Harry Griffiths in the early 1980s in his 'Radio Shack'

---

* Given that The Cambridge Five passed copious amounts of intelligence on to their Soviet minders during the war, it is hardly surprising that Harry was being monitored by the Russians.

Some Inconvenient Facts...

IN THE INTRODUCTION to Nigel West's book GCHQ, he makes some interesting observations.(1)

GCHQ had two particular worries:

Firstly - it didn't want it to be known that the Allies had discovered successful decryption was almost entirely dependent on extremely accurate interception. The discovery of cribs, and most important of all, minor mistakes made even by the most skilled enemy radio operators, oft times helped enormously. Used correctly, the Enigma Machines' codes were unbreakable; errors were literally the key to cryptanalytical success. (The Allies wanted their success to be attached to military might alone.)

Secondly - GCHQ became concerned with the fate of many thousands of Enigma Machines recovered from Germany in 1945. Hunting for these Machines became a popular past time for signals personnel after the surrender. The reward for finding a Machine intact was a home leave pass. The purpose of collecting them was to have them reconditioned and to offer them to friendly governments as a means of secure communications. Even in the 1970s, many of these Machines were in use across the world. (Of course the ability of Bletchley to readily read these messages would not have been known!) Bletchley Park came into the public domain in the early 1980s and only then would it have become apparent to our wartime Allies that Britain had not told the truth concerning the 'security' of the Enigma Machines!

NB: Gordon Welchman makes the same assertions in his book – 'The Hut Six Story', (2)

Roll of Honour

BLETCHLY PARK HAS now produced a medal recognising service in support of their work during WW2. It is estimated that well over 10,000 personnel were involved in the work at Bletchley, together with its many outstations.

However, for deceased veterans, a digital medal has been awarded which their relatives can access on the Bletchley Park website.

The original organisation that ran Bletchley Park was the Government Code & Cypher School and GC&CS is impressed on the medal.

A Roll of Honour has been produced by the Bletchley Park Trust and the intention is that all personnel will eventually have their names added.

To date, only 42 St Erth staff have had their names recorded on the roll. If you wish to add a name to this Roll of Honour, the author suggests that you should contact the Bletchley Park Trust.

Name	Service	Call Sign	Where served
Abbott Ken	Army		St Erth RSS SCU3
Andrews Jack	GPO civilian then Army from1942		Lydd Aug – Sept 1940 St Erth March 1947 HF/DF Op
Ayres Tom	Army		St Erth RSS SCU3
Carter W	Army		Arkley & St Erth RSS SCU3 DF Central Switch Board
Chamberlain Joe	Army		St Erth RSS SCU3
Cornish Ron	Army		St Erth RSS SCU3 DF
Cox Arthur Henry	Army		Gilnahirk, St Erth & Thurso 1942-45 Inter Op
Edwards George	RSS civilian then Army	G2UX	RSS VI Hanslope later Wymondham & St Erth DF
Finch Charles	Army		St Erth RSS SCU3
Galpin Reginald E	Army	GW2FWD	Hanslope, Belfast, Gilnahirk & St Erth RSS June 1944 – Oct 1946 SCU3
Garton Ron	RSS civilian then Army		Hanslope & St Erth RSS SCU3 VI
Griffiths Harry	GPO civilian then Army from 1943	G2DFH	St Erth RSS SCU3 DF
Groves Stan	RSS civilian then Army		St Erth RSS SCU3

Name	Service	Call Sign	Where served
Hanlon Jimmy	Army		St Erth RSS SCU3
Howarth Ted	RSS civilian then Army		St Erth RSS SCU3 & SCU4 VI
McAfferty John	Army		St Erth RSS to 1943 then Lydd SCU3 DF
McCafferty John	RSS civilian later Army		St Erth RSS SCU3
MacLeod Don	Army		St Erth RSS SCU3 DF
Middleton Ken	Army	G2NL	St Erth 1939 – 1941. Arkley 1941 – 1943 RSS SCU3
Moore Archie	Army		St Erth RSS SCU3
Nobbs Danny	Army		St Erth RSS SCU3
Oaks Arthur	Army		St Erth RSS SCU3
Orr James	Army	G8J0	Hanslope Park & St Erth RSS SCU3 DF
Ottery Kenneth	Army	G3ECS	St Erth RSS SCU3
Pace Ernie G	Army		Arkley & St Erth Jan 1944 – June 1946 RSS SCU3 Tele Op
Price Eddie	Army		St Erth RSS SCU3
Ranner Brian	Army		St Erth RSS SCU3
Reid Kenneth J	Army		Arkley Jan – May 1944 St Erth June 1944 – Jan 1946 SCU3 Inter Op
Rigg Harry	Army		St Erth RSS SCU3
Robertson John	Army		St Erth RSS SCU3
Ross Ken	Army		Arkley & St Erth RSS SCU3
Smith William	Army		Arkley & St Erth RSS SCU3 & Alexandria SCU4
Snowden Roy	Army		St Erth RSS SCU3
Tough Alex	Army		Arkley & St Erth RSS SCU3
Turner George	Army		St Erth RSS SCU3
Wallis Donald F	Army		St Erth June 1943 – Feb 1944 then Middle East Radio Service SCU3 & 4 Inter Op
Ward Geoff	Army		Arkley & St Erth RSS SCU3
Westren Frank	Army		St Erth RSS SCU3 Sidi Bishr SCU4
Wherry Reg	Army		St Erth RSS SCU3
Whitehead Harry	Army		Gilnahirk, Thurso 1941 – 43 Forfar 1943 – 46 and St Erth SCU 3 Inter Op
Whittaker H	Army	G3SJ	St Erth RSS SCU3
Yule Leslie	Army		Arkley & St Erth RSS SCU3

Appendix

- The POW Camp at St Erth — a POW's Story
- St Erth home Guard

My thanks to Di Webber for this photo of the camp, taken by her late husband Russell; he took this in the early 1990s, not long before the site was cleared

Mike Millichamp provided this aerial picture from the early 1990s

An interesting picture, thanks to John Hobson. It was taken sometime in the 1950s from the back bedroom of his parents' home and shows the camp covered in snow, behind the line of trees

Appendix I

St Erth Prisoner of War Camp – A POW's Story

THANKS TO THE research of the late Russell Webber, locally much is now known about the POW camp at St Erth and it is not my intention to repeat what is widely available. However, as always happens when you research around a subject, you find some interesting nuggets. One odd fact is that the camp at St Erth seems not to be on any official lists of such sites around the country.

Experiences of a boy from Bietzefeld

As was common practice throughout the UK – the more trustworthy German/Italian prisoners were put to work in local industries or, indeed, anywhere where help was needed and St Erth was no exception. The following narrative is the story of man who was known in the village as 'John the German'.

Jann Kampen – 'John', began to work in 1946 at Tredrea Manor, which was farmed by Mr Wilfred Harry and his family. Following the eventual release of all POWs, John was offered bed and board at Tredrea for as long as he wanted it. He only returned home to Germany once – to attend his sister's wedding in 1953. He maintained that his old home had changed post-war and he preferred the peace of his new life on the farm in West Cornwall. He was a trained Blacksmith and his skill to make and mend anything was very evident in my memory of him. My family knew him well; he was a most charming and gentle man with a ready smile, his German/Cornish dialect was and is, unforgettable.

Jann 'John' Folkert Kampen in his early 20s (1924–2017)

During the summer of 2012, John's nephew came to Tredrea to record his life story. I am indebted to Doe Harry for allowing me to reproduce it here – as it was recorded at that time. It is a very moving account of one man's experience as he passes through the various theatres of war. The single line entries are a commentary on a world reeling from the devastating consequences of five plus years of the bloodiest conflict known to history. Almost every line seems to touch on major world events and attitudes.

Experiences of a boy from Bietzefeld in WW11 and thereafter

Name: Jann Kampen, born on the 9th of June 1924, in Bietzefeld, close to Holtrop

1939-1942	Apprenticeship to be a blacksmith in Holtrop.
December 1942	Conscription papers, departure from Bietzefeld to a place close to Rostock. Received clothing, stayed approximately a week - departure by train to Esbert, Denmark, to take part in basic military training. Learnt to ride horses because I was apparently fit to work with horses as a trained blacksmith. There, they held a small Christmas celebration. Did not enjoy the work with horses.
Spring 1943	Transferred to Miramas close to Marseille in France. Horses were trained to get used to"…" artillery. Before the Germans were stationed there, there were Italians which were not in favour with the French. Transport of bigger units to that place, (at least 100 horses).
Summer 1943	Transferred to the Eastern Front to Poltawa and Charkow (Ukraine). Their journey leads them through Southern Germany. In Poltawa, there are no plastered roads only dirt roads. There were 8 horses in one coach and two caretakers slept in between the horses. The front was calm. In a village, I met a Russian girl. She mend (?)his socks and did not seem to be afraid. North of Poltawa around Kursk, there was a battle of tanks. After that, days of withdrawal but only once under fire from the Russian air force. A lot of walking, crossing of river Dniepr. There, the Russians closed in. At that time, I fell ill with Malaria. Sergeant took the sick to the soldiers' lazaret. From hospital, I was moved by truck to a train station and was 10 days on the move to the West up to Koniggratz (Czechoslovakia). Saw the Carpathian Mountains on the way. Treatment against Malaria but not in a hospital. Less than 50 kg of weight, eating glucose, received quinine pills. Via Praha and Berlin home. Arrival in December 1943. At the blacksmith in Holtrop (former employer). I met Russian soldiers from Stalingrad.
Just before Xmas 1943	Back to Rostock, where he worked on the train service, reloaded post for Finland, (Approx 1 month).
January 1944	Transferred to Munster – had good times there. (1 week)
Spring 1944	Transferred to Brittany, train station Morlay (?), marching to…..another Malana attack close to Lond….. (?) Party of German officers. Drunk officer aimed at me (I was on watch), I aimed back at him but did not shoot. Russian soldier as partner for work with the horses for the (?) Transferred to the coast and again to the Normandy.
6ᵗʰ June 1944	The unit was put together but they did not leave for the Normandy.
End of July 1944	Transferred to St Lo, Normandy. Under fire on the way to support the fighting troops. After that, withdrawal of the troops always by night because of the raids by the RAF. Saw one French civilian get killed in an air raid. Withdrawal to Falaise - Argentan.
	There all the horses that I had to take care of were killed. Then, hiding in trenches. Americans were calling on them "Hands up, don't shoot". I took a white handkerchief and waived. After that more comrades came out of hiding. At that time the Americans had already conquered Paris. In the Normandy, the Germans were closed in. We were taken prisoner while it was pouring with rain. The next morning, we got some chocolate from the Americans. I met a wounded sergeant from my unit. From Normandy, we went in landing boats to Northern England, in a camp near Mansfield, Nottingham. From the closest harbour, we went to

America in a ship convoy. On the way, there were 2 alarms because of German submarines. Arrival in New York, driving past the Statue of Liberty. The journey continues on a train towards a region around the Mississippi.

8th May 1945	End of war in Europe. For a while, there was less food available but in general, we were treated well as POWs in the different camps:
Camp Clinton:	Close to Clarksdale, south of Memphis, Tenn. – 8 hours a day digging up tree roots but not every day - 6 days a week.
Camp Shelby:	Lived in tents, worked in laundrette (ironing uniforms) and/or picked cotton. Received 1$ a day, black people received less. They lived in huts that were in worse condition than the tents of the POW.
Camp McCain:	Sunday cinema with Bing Crosby, 2 friends from the Ruhr area in Germany, some of (............) the companions stay in the USA.
March/April 46	Departure from USA by boat from New York (we thought that we would go home). Arrival in a camp in Bruges, Belgium. There, lived under bad living conditions, no food for nearly one month. We could hardly walk we were so weak, nearly died of hunger. A DP (Displaced Person), (probably someone from Lithuania, Estonia or Latvia, who was called into the German Army), betrayed when trading dollar for food. He kept the money but did not bring the bread. After a complaint to the Red Cross, the camp was closed. On the last day, there was enough soup for everyone. After that, boat trip on a rough sea, the conditions on board were horrendous.
26th May 1946	Arrival in England (written document exists) in harbour of Plymouth. Trip continues to a camp close to St Erth, Penzance Cornwall. There, I lived in the camp and worked daily with other POWs on Mr Harry's farm. For the first time during my time as soldier, the children who were playing in the sand did not run away from the German soldiers. In all other countries, the children ran away. These children did not know the war. The meals were taken separately from the family in the beginning. After a couple of weeks, we were allowed to walk to work to work by ourselves. After some months, the Harry's take me on the farm. The three Harry daughters look on me as their older brother.
15th Nov 1947	The POW'S are discharged in Camborne, close to Hayle, Cornwall, (the document exists). Since then - I am in England a civilian.
22nd Dec 1948	Discharged (?) (Existing document).
30th Apr - 2nd Jun 1953	First and only visit to Germany because of my sister's wedding (German passport of the German embassy in London, existing document). Former friends did not show a lot of interest in talking. The return flight was already booked.
Since then:	Living and working with the Harry family, now sharing a cottage next to the farm with Doris Harry. Receive a small pension from Germany as well as in UK.

Jann Kampen, St Erth, Cornwall, UK
Written down: Jann Campen during his visit 9-19th June 2012

As the previous page details, John stayed in a number of camps as a prisoner; one such camp was Camp Clinton, Mississippi, USA. This photograph makes it look very palatial in comparison to the St Erth Camp

John at
Tredrea Farm
– 1960s

Doris (Doe) Harry, David Griffiths, Jann Folkert 'John' Kampen and the Author 5th September 2008

Appendix II

St Erth Home Guard 1940-43

DURING MAY 1940, the Secretary of State for War, Anthony Eden, announced the formation of the Local Defence Volunteers (LDV) over the radio and called for men to enlist. As a result, the St Erth platoon was formed during that summer – comprised of men who were either too young or too old to go to war, or of a reserved occupation.

The country wide force grew to over 1.5 million with the aim to inhibit any invasion attempts by the enemy. It was Churchill who, on becoming Prime Minister, decided to change the name of the LDV to the Home Guard.*

During my general research into wartime St Erth, a resident and family friend showed me a note book from that period. It held all the details of the local HG and every aspect of kit that was issued to an individual was recorded therein. Mr W F Bew (the village schoolmaster) was the Quartermaster Sergeant (QMS).

According to this book there were 60 men enlisted on the 10th of March 1941. The principle officers of the platoon were:

Platoon Commander	F A Bewes
Section Commander	E James
Section Leaders	J Stone
" "	C H Dodd
" "	W Warren
" "	W F Bew QMS

St Erth Home Guard 1941. Back row: Jim Hart, Jack Hart, W Harris, H Nance, H Matthews, R Eddy, C Pellow, M Hancock, E Lashbrook and W Matthews. Middle row: H Nicholas, G O Taylor, M Thomas, S Bond, D Lugg, H Taylor, I Eckers, E Harris and A Johns. Front row: S Lugg, W Ran, W Warren, W F Bew, F Bunn, E Jenkin, C Dodd, I Stone, L Treglown, L Oates and J Heather

---

* Malicious tongues said that LDV stood for 'Look, Duck and Vanish'.

The document also listed the positions of the three observation posts, they were:

The Post Office – (The Alarm Post)
seen here (with the bay window) at the end of the street

The Bridge – (Where the Molotov cocktails were buried)

Between Carnabeggas (above) and Esmeralda, at the top of St Erth Hill –
(two large houses near to the radio station)

List of Platoon Members

Each member of the HG had his kit recorded. (Ernest Harris was our step grandfather, residing at Pendennis, St Erth.)

Raids and Warnings

The original page is very faint, so I have extracted some entries for clarity. This list records every time the siren sounded, heralding a possible sighting of enemy aircraft. St Erth was machine gunned on 7th January 1941, but the police reported that there was no damage or casualties. Four HE bombs were dropped on the lane between Tredrea and Trewinard Farm during the night of 1st August 1941. I recall my mother telling our family that on that night, she heard an enemy bomber being chased by a fighter plane, prior to the bombs exploding. The spot where they exploded was often pointed out when our family walked up the lane on a Sunday afternoon stroll.

Year 1940 Entries

Month	Day	Time	
Sept	20th	10:45 – 11:10 AM	
Oct	1st	09:20 – 09:40 AM	
Oct	1st	09:10 – 10:15 PM	
Oct	2nd	07:30 – damage done	
Oct	9th	07:45 – 08:30 PM	
Oct	9th	09:55 – 10:15 PM	a busy evening (authors comment!)
Oct	9th	10:35 – 10:50 PM	

Primrose Dairy Home Guard

There was another Home Guard in the vicinity with an unlikely name!

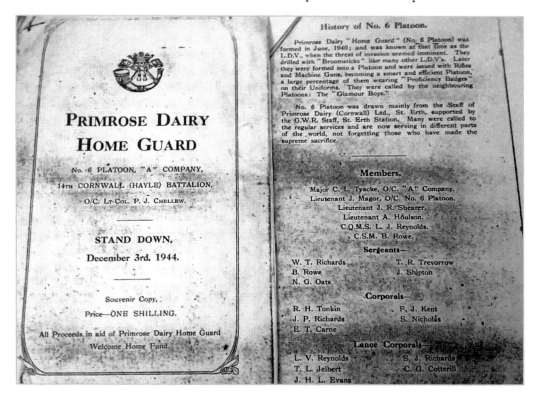

PRIMROSE DAIRY HOME GUARD

No. 6 PLATOON, "A" COMPANY,
14TH CORNWALL (HAYLE) BATTALION,
O/C. LT-COL. P. J. CHELLEW.

STAND DOWN,
December 3rd, 1944.

Souvenir Copy,
Price—ONE SHILLING.

All Proceeds in aid of Primrose Dairy Home Guard
Welcome Home Fund.

History of No. 6 Platoon.

Primrose Dairy "Home Guard" (No. 6 Platoon) was formed in June, 1940; and was known at that time as the L.D.V., when the threat of invasion seemed imminent. They drilled with "Broomsticks" like many other L.D.V's. Later they were formed into a Platoon and were issued with Rifles and Machine Guns, becoming a smart and efficient Platoon, a large percentage of them wearing "Proficiency Badges" on their Uniforms. They were called by the neighbouring Platoons: The "Glamour Boys."

No. 6 Platoon was drawn mainly from the Staff of Primrose Dairy (Cornwall) Ltd., St. Erth, supported by the G.W.R. Staff, St. Erth Station. Many were called to the regular services and are now serving in different parts of the world, not forgetting those who have made the supreme sacrifice.

Members.

Major C. L. Tyacke, O.C. "A" Company.
Lieutenant J. Magor, O.C. No. 6 Platoon.
Lieutenant J. R. Shearer.
Lieutenant A. Houlson.
C.Q.M.S. L. J. Reynolds.
C.S.M. B. Rowe.

Sergeants—

W. T. Richards	T. R. Trevorrow
B. Rowe	J. Shipton
N. G. Oats	

Corporals—

R. H. Tonkin	F. J. Kent
J. P. Richards	S. Nicholas
E. T. Carne	

Lance Corporals—

L. V. Reynolds	S. J. Richards
T. L. Jelbert	C. G. Cotterill
J. H. L. Evans	

Privates—

P. Pascoe	R. J. Sampson
R. Francis	R. D. Seccombe
R. K. Hutchens	J. L. Thomas
R. H. Francis	T. C. Tregear
L. Curnow	T. J. Tregear
M. Harvey	S. A. Trevorrow
D. Trembath	W. T. W. Uren
R. Giles	J. R. Vincent
W. J. Sedgman	C. K. H. Yendle
R. Tinkley	W. H. Williams
R. T. Bawden	M. P. Stone
H. Blewett	Killed on Active Service
W. H. Botheras	W. G. L. Bailey
J. A. Broad	O. Edwards
W. Burr	S. A. Mills
J. Chapple	N. K. Andrews
C. Curnow	R. J. Williams
A. C. Dunkley	R. Woolcock
W. F. D. Gall	S. H. Richards
T. Hattam	V. Hall
B. Hocking	H. A. Tregenza
H. Hollow	R. J. Rowe
W. R. Hollow	A. K. Hurrell
E. G. James	A. C. Leeves
C. James	F. Sanders
W. R. Jenkin	A. C. Rowe
A. J. Lawrey	T. A. Williams
C. Mungles	S. Blewett
E. J. Murley	R. J. Richards
J. B. Nankervis	J. C. Noble
G. L. Osborne	F. W. Thomas
J. S. Richards	R. Date
E. Rowe	R. H. Harris
P. Sampson	

*On Active Service.

Farewell to Primrose Dairy Platoon.

No more shall we hear the whistle
Calling us on Parade ;
No more excuses have we — — ·
To make, or Drills we might evade.

Don't give us that " stuff " any more, " Albert " !
We just won't listen to you, see !
And " Jackie " you can polish
That " tooth " 'cos Brasso's going to be free !

A guy called " Grigg " has told us
We can keep our " greatcoats " see,
But *you* can't keep your " pips ",
Because " pips " aren't going to be free,

Some have to walk to work these days,
There's no more " Home Guard " juice,
While we can wear our " Home Guard " boots,
Although they pinch like the " Duce."

No more shall our nightly
Vigils be disturbed by " 'Phoney Calls,"
To ask for Mr. " So and So " because
He won't be " on call."

" Primrose Dairy " can turn them out
" Lousy " with talent, there's no doubt,
Majors, Captains, " Pips " galore,
Enough to frighten any foe.

We've paddled through the mud and slime,
While some stood on the brink,
We thought we'd lost our " Georgie "
Some-one saw him sink.

We've crawled until our knees are sore,
Now they don't want us any more,
These " Glamour Boys " of No. Six
Who played " O' Grady " all for nix!

We ought to have a " Flag Day "
For the Boys with " Housemaid's Knees,"
Or Private " Gall " might give us
All the profit from his " Bees."

So Goodbye to " No. 6 Platoon,"
We think you've finished all too soon ! ! !
From the " Major " to the " Private,"
We'll meet in a warmer Climate.

L/Cpl. S. J. RICHARDS.

With apologies to Lieuts. J. MAGOR and A. HOULSON.

I am grateful to the Lashbrook family for this memory of their father – Eslea.

"Our father's main role in the Home Guard was as a Lance Jack. He had to guard a mortar gun and a store of 20 Molotov cocktails buried in the ground close to the bridge. He said that if the Germans invaded Cornwall, then the job of the St Erth platoon was to defend the bridge at all costs. Fortunately, that occasion never materialised and the bombs were removed at the end of the war.

Eslea Lashbrook post-war

"He took his role in the Home Guard very seriously and found his work, duty/balance very difficult to achieve. As a blacksmith, he worked a very long day mending farm implements and shoeing horses and then, most evenings, he had to find the energy to carry out his Home Guard duties. As well as guarding the bridge, he also would have had to do a turn at the top of St Erth Hill. One evening an officer came and advised him that he could not be in charge of the mortar unless he was made a full corporal, but this promotion was something that father did not want, so he refused.

"On his next duty at the station, the officer came again and gave him his corporal stripes, but he refused to wear them. He was then threatened with Court Martial. Later, he received a letter from Headquarters informing him he was to be reduced to the ranks. At the end of hostilities he received his Certificate of Thanks from King George VI for his wartime service."

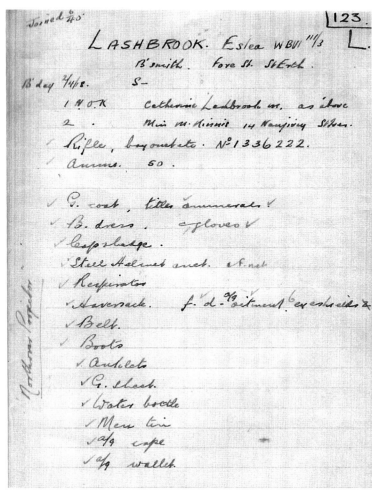

Acknowledgements and Thanks

THIS BOOK HAS been quite a journey; seldom had a week gone by without another piece of the jigsaw coming to light. I am indebted and give thanks to the following for their help, suggestions, insightful comments, knowledge and enthusiasm without which this narrative would not have been possible:

Stan Ames, the Archivist of the RSS, whose technical history and organisational knowledge helped me to make sense of all things radio and more. The late Bob King, a veteran of the RSS, who interpreted nets from Harry's Code Book. Barrie Smith of Townsend, who pieced together the facts relating to the underground tank at Mably Farm. The Holness brothers and Leonard Green who confirmed this Ultra Secret site. Di Webber, whose late husband Russell's research added much to the detail of the main radio station site and also for his knowledge of the POW Camp. The late Frank Western, who was the only veteran I met who actually worked at the station. The late Mary Curnow and her family, whose memories and photographs added to my narrative.

The following, whose late fathers worked at the station: Margaret Woolcock, the daughter, of Jimmy Hanlon, who contributed her memories; Susan Hutton provided the history and photographs of her father Ken Reid; Rod MacLeod – son of Sgt Don MacLeod – gave both narrative and photographs; Derek Moore shared the story of his father Archie.

I would also like to thank Doe Harry, a lifelong friend of the family, who still lives in St Erth and helped to organise my talks in the village, from which a number of valuable contacts emerged. The late Jann Kampen – 'John the German' – who was a resident of the POW camp, for the copy of his life story. My brothers – David and Edward and my sister Blanche, whose collective memories helped enormously. Jess Slocombe, of Bretonside Copy, for her advice and for patiently completing the alterations and corrections to my narrative.

Finally, my wife Pearl, who was my constant, without her ideas, encouragement and continued enthusiasm there would have been no book! and my children John and Nicola, who have given me unstinted support throughout and have weathered all things 'Bletchley'.

In conclusion, my sincere thanks and apologies to those people that I have omitted. I take full responsibility for any mistakes or omissions that may be apparent in this narrative. Inevitably, there has been an amount of joining up of dots, but I hope that, ultimately, my account is a fitting memorial to the many who served their country at St Erth Radio Station.

Michael Griffiths
Spring 2024

Photographic Credits

Whilst every effort has been made to contact copyright holders, much is from the Public domain and from a time period when finding the holder has not proven to be possible.

Wireless War	GPO Archives
General Guderian	Bundesarchiv Bild 104-769-0229-12A/CC-BY-SA/3.0

WHERE IT ALL BEGAN
<u>A Scouser Goes West</u>

Aerial Photograph	Cornwall County Planning
G2DFH (QSL Card)	Trevor Goldsworthy
Marconi Morse Key	Wilson family

<u>The Main Radio Station Site</u>

Map DDP59/2/15/17	Kresen Kernow
Aerial photograph	Cornwall County Planning
Inside the Interception hut	Bob King

<u>The Underground Tank at Mably Farm</u>

Aerial photograph	Cornwall County Planning
Sequence of underground tank	Stan Ames RSS Archivist
Photograph of top of underground tank	Stan Ames RSS Archivist
Internal view of underground tank	Stan Ames RSS Archivist

<u>The Bletchley Web</u>

Bletchley Park	Public Domain
German HQ	Pinterest

THE CODE BOOK

Hugh Trevor Roper	Creative Commons Wikimedia
Enigma Machine	Public Domain
RSS Log Sheet	Bob King
Nauen Transmitter	Creative Commons, Wikimedia
B-24 Liberator	Creative Commons, Wikimedia
FFF dossier	The National Archives
Agent ZigZag	Military Intelligence 5
Radio Net	Bletchley Park Trust
The Man Who Never Was	Ronald Neame
Himmler	Creative Commons: *Bundesarchiv, Bild 183-S 72707/ CC-BY-SA 3.0*
Letter of commendation	Vera Quick
Tirpitz photograph	Creative Commons: *Bundesarchiv, Bild 183-J19316/Boeckmann/CC-BY-SA 30*
Sebold & Duquesne	FBI
Centreport Long Island	FBI

Frank Henneberg	Henneberg family
QSL card	Henneberg family
Most Secret letter	Stan Ames
The House on 92nd Street	Jerry Murbach
	(www.doctormaco.com)
Bill & Helen Sebold	Shirley Camerer
Frank Henneberg & wife	Henneberg family
Italian Submarine Barbarigo	Public Domain Wikipedia
Capitano di Corvetta Enzo Grossi	Public Domain Wikipedia
Bordeaux Submarine Pens	Creative Commons
Bismarck photograph	Creative Commons:
	Bundesarchiv,
	Bild 193-04-1-26/CC-BY-
	SA-30

THE BIG PICTURE

Double Cross

Agent Garbo	Military Intelligence 5
Agent Treasure	The National Archives
Agent Tricycle	Public Domain Wikipedia
Agent Brutus	Public Domain Wikipedia
Agent Snow	Public Domain
Agent Tate	Fair use Wikipedia org
Wilhelm Canaris	Creative Commons
	Wikimedia
Halina Szymanski	Public Domain

Luminaries of Bletchley Park

Marian Adam Rejewski	Creative Commons
	Wikimedia
Alan Turing	Public Domain Wikipedia
Gordon Welchman	Fair Use Wikipedia org
Bill Tutte	Youlden family
Tommy Flowers	Public Domain Wikipedia

The Cambridge 5

Philby	Fair Use Wikipedia org
Cairncross	Fair Use Wikipedia org
Blunt	Fair Use Wikipedia org

Voluntary Interceptors

Gambier-Parry	Fair Use Wikipedia org
Radio Security Service World Wide	Stan Ames RSS Archivist
RSS Log Sheet	Bob King
Radio Equipment	Bob King

STATION ANECDOTES

Stories Behind the Faces

Ken Reid	Susan Hutton
Archie Moore	Derek Moore
Titanic	Public Domain
Charles Lightholler	Public Domain
SS California	Public Domain
Don MacLeod	Rod MacLeod
DF Hut	Rod MacLeod

Sylvia Goldsworthy	Sylvia Rule
Frank Westren	Westren Family
Jimmy Hanlon	Margaret Woolcock
Photographs of staff	Susan Hutton & Rod MacLeod
Thurso site	Stan Ames RSS Archivist
Harry Locket	Curnow family
Radio Equipment Store	Shirley Thompson
Aerial array	Rod MacLeod
DF hut during the war	Rod MacLeod
Thurso site	Stan Ames RSS Archivist
Hexagonal hut	Graham Hill
Leonard Green at field entrance	Barrie Smith
The Guard Hut	Barrie Smith
Mary Curnow	Curnow family
St Erth War Memorial	George Pritchard

POST WAR

Picture of GCHQ Bude	Creative Commons Wikimedia
Trawler	Public Domain
Avro Shackelton	RAF Museum

APPENDIX

Prisoner of War Camp

Jann (John) Kampen	Doe Harry
John at Tredrea	Doe Harry & Clive Rodda

Home Guard

The St Erth Platoon	Public Domain
The Post Office	Rod MacLeod
The Bridge	Edward Griffiths
Eslea Lashbrook	Lashbrook family
Back page	Royal British Legion

Notes and Sources

A Scouser Goes West
1 I Cobain, the History Thieves. p137

The Underground Tank at Mably Farm Townsend
1 Gerry Openshaw's audio recordings at the Imperial War Museum site 1990
    https://www.iwm.org.uk/collections/item/object/80011469 Reel 4

The Bletchley Web
1 G Busby, The Spies at Gilnahirk. p122

The Code Book
1 Gerry Openshaw's audio recordings at the Imperial War Museum site 1990
    https://www.iwm.org.uk/collections/item/object/80011469 Reel 4
2 H.T Roper, The Secret World. p12
3 H.T Roper, The Wartime Journals. p93
4 K Beauchamp, History of Telegraphy 2001
5 M Paterson, Codebreakers. p148
6 N Booth, ZigZag. p107, D Abrutat, Radio War. p162

Preambles and Group Numbers
1G Welchman, The Hut Six Story. p154
2 Ibid p56
3 Ibid p35
4 Ibid p225
5 Ibid p158
6 G Pidgeon, The Secret Wireless War. p103
7 H.T. Roper, The Secret World. p37
8 F Hinsley, British Intell in WW2 Vol 4. p301
9 G Welchman, The Hut Six Story. p93
10 F Hinsley, British Intell in WW2 Vol 3 part 1. p78 & p120
11 N West, GCHQ. p174
12 Ibid p178
13 R Lewin, Ultra Goes To War. p118
14 M Hastings, The Secret War. p545

Group 2 The Norway Net
1 J Levine, Operation Fortitude. p226
2 Ibid p210
3 Ibid p57
4 H.T Roper, The Secret World. p2
5 K Jeffery, MI6. p518
6 F Hinsley, British Intell in WW2 Vol 3 part1. p259
7 J Jackson, Code Wars. p120-33
8 M Hastings, The Secret War. P214

Group 10 The American Connection
1 P Duffy, Double Agent. p112
2 Ibid p139

3 Fritz Joubert Duquesne, FBI
4 P Duffy, Double Agent. p175

Italian Sub-Codes
1 G Hill, Unpublished Dissertation, DF the Bismarck & Italian Navy.
2 K Moeller LCDR USN, Italian Submarine Forces in the Atlantic WW2 2010
3 Ibid
4 RAF St Eval – Wikipedia
5 G Hill, Unpublished Dissertation, DF the Bismarck & Italian Navy
6 G Busby, The Spies at Gilnahirk. p122

The Double Cross System
1 J C Masterman, Double Cross System
2 J Webster, The Spy With 29 Names & NA KV2/40
3 L Serqueier, Secret Service Rendered & NA KV2/466
4 R Miller, Code Name Tricycle & NA KV2/859
5 B Macintyre, The Secret Hero of D-Day Times Newspaper Jan 2018 & NA KV2/73
6 J Hayward, Double Agent Snow & NA KV2/444
7 Jonason Olsson, Agent Tate & NA KV2/61
8 N Booth, ZigZag & NA KV2/456
9 R Bassett, Hitler's Spy Chief, Cassell Military Paperbacks 2005

The Luminaries of Bletchley Park
1 Crypto Museum.Com
2 J S Ciechanowski, Living with the Enigma Secret 2005
3 "Poles finally honoured for cracking Enigma Code", The Times Sept 2021
4 Alan Turing, GCHQ
5 Stephen Budiansky, The Battle of Wits 2000
6 A Hodges, Alan Turing
7 G Welchman, The Hut Six Story
8 BBC Documentary 2015, BP Code Breaking Forgotten Genius
9 R Denniston, Gordon Welchman 2004
10 BBC News, Bill Tute, September 2014
11 Capt Jerry Roberts, Lorenz, The History Press
12 Tommy Flowers, History Learning Site.co.uk

The Cambridge Five
1 BBC Radio 4, 4th April 2016, The Cambridge Five
2 N West, MI6. p306 (Lisbon)
3 H Philby, My Silent War. p53
4 N West, The Crown Jewels. p294 The Philiby Report
5 M Smith, Anatomy of a Traitor. p236 Details of Post Office
6 Ibid p242, Details of Radio Traffic
7 A Christopher, The Defence of the Realm. p441
8 Ibid p706, Thatcher
9 History Today, 17th Oct 2016, recent release from the NA
10 BBC Panorama, How Many More Skeletons 2nd Nov 1981

Post–War Some Inconvenient Facts
1 N West, GCHQ. p22
2 G Welchman, The Hut Six Story. p17

Select Bibliography

Abrutat David, *Radio Wars*, Fonthill 2019

Aldrich R J, *GCHQ*, Harper Press 2011

Andrew C, *The Authorised History of MI5*, Penguin Books 2009

Bamford J, *The Puzzle Palace*, Penguin Books 1983

Bassett R, *Hitler's Spy Chief*, Cassell Military Paperbacks 2005

Bennett R, *Ultra in the West*, Scribner's Sons 1980

Bletchley Park Home of the Codebreakers, Pitkin Publishing 2014

Booth Nicholas, *ZigZag*, Piatus Books Ltd 2007

Budiansky S, *Battle of Wits*, Penguin 2000

Busby G, *The Spies at Gilnahirk*, Ballyhay Books 2016

Carter Miranda, *Anthony Blunt: His Lives*, Pan Macmillan 2001

Cobain I, *The History Thieves*, Portobello Books 2017

Dimbleby J, *The Battle of the Atlantic*, Penguin 2015

Duffy P, *Double Agent*, Scribner 2014

Farago L, *The Game of the Foxes*, Book Club Ass. 1971

Gannon P, *Colossus Bletchley Parks Greatest Secret*, Atlantic Books 2006

Garcia & West, *Operation Garbo*, CPI Group (UK), Ltd 1985

Harper S, *Capturing the Enigma*, Sutton Publishing 1999

Hastings M, *The Secret War*, William Collins 2015

Hayward J, *Double Agent Snow*, Simon & Schuster 2013

Hinsley Thomas, *Ransom & Knight British Intelligence in the Second World War, Vol 3,* HMSO 1984

Hinsley & Simkins, *British Intelligence in the Second World War, Vol 4,* HMSO 1990

Hodges A, *Alan Turing: The Enigma*, Vintage 2014

Jackson J, *Code Wars*, Pen & Sword Military 2011

Jeffery K, *MI6, The History of the Secret Intelligence Service*, Bloomsbury 2010

Jonason & Olsson, *Agent Tate*, Amberley 2011

Jones R V, *Most Secret War*, Hodder and Stoughton 1978

Kahn D, *Seizing the Enigma*, Arrow 1991

Levine J, Operation Fortitude, Collins 2012

Lewin R, *Ultra Goes to War*, Arrow 2008

Macintyre B, *AGENT ZIGZAG*, Bloomsbury 2007

Macintyre B, *A Spy Among Friends (Philby),* Bloomsbury 2014

Macintyre B, *Double Cross*, Bloomsbury 2012

Macintyre B, *Operation Mincemeat*, Bloomsbury 2010

Macksey K, *The Searchers*, Sharpe Books 2003

McKay S, *The Secret Life of Bletchley Park*, Aurum 2010

McKay S, *The Secret Listeners*, Aurum 2012

Masterman J C, *The Double Cross System*, The Lyons Press 2000

Matthews P, *SIGINT*, The History Press 2013

Miller R, *Codename TRICYCLE*, Random House 2004

Montefiore-Sebag H, *Enigma*, Phoenix 2000

Paterson M, *Voices of the Codebreakers*, David & Charles 2007

Philby K, *My Silent War*, Random House 2002

Pidgeon G, *The Secret Wireless War*, Arundel Books 2008

Pincher C, *Treachery*, Random House 2009

Roper H T, *The Secret World*, Tauris & Co 2014

Roper H T, *The Wartime Journals*, Tauris & Co 2012
Sergueiev L, *Secret Service Rendered*, Kimber 1966
Smith C, *The Last Cambridge Spy*, The History Press 2019
Smith G, *Devon & Cornwall Airfields in the Second World War*,
Countryside Books 2000
Smith M, *The Anatomy of a Traitor*, Aurum Press 2017
Smith M, *The Secrets of Station X*, Biteback Publishing 2011
Sullivan B, *Hayle in World War 2*, The St Ives Printing & Publishing Comp. 2011
Turing D, *Bletchley Park, Demystifying the Bombe*, Pitkin Publishing 2014
Webber R, *Unpublished Research Papers of St Erth Radio Station & POW Camp*
1990s
Webster J, *The Spy With 29 Names*, Chatto & Windus 2014
Welchman G, *The Hut Six Story*, M&M Baldwin 2011
West N, *Double Cross in Cairo*, Biteback Publishing 2015
West N, *GCHQ*, Hodder & Stoughton 1986
West N, MI6, Hodder & Stoughton 1985
West N, & Oleg Tsarev, *The Crown Jewels*, HarperCollins 1998
Winterbotham F, *The Ultra Secret*, Futura Publications Ltd 1974

DVD
Rixan D & D, *The Secret Wireless War*, Grindelwald 2002

Web Page
East Anglian Film Archive: Wartime Radio: Secret Listeners 1979
St Erth Welcome Web Page: select 'About St Erth' then the WWII file.
Gerry Openshaw's audio recordings at the Imperial War Museum site 1990:
https://www.iwm.org.uk/collections/item/object/80011469
www.secretlisteners.org

Abbreviations

BP	Bletchley Park
CS	Call Sign
DF	Direction Finding
EN CLAIR	Written in plain speech - rather than in code
FBI	Federal Bureaux of Investigation
GCHQ	Government Communications Headquarters
GC & CS	Government Code & Cypher School
Gestapo	The German Nazi Party's Secret Police
GPO	General Post Office
HF/DF	High Frequency Direction Finding – also known as Huff Duff
HG	Home Guard
Iron Curtain	Churchill's name for the Soviet Union's border with Western Europe post WW2
MI5	Military Intelligence 5 - British Security Service
MI6	Military Intelligence 6 - British Secret Intelligence Service (also SIS)
MI8	Military Intelligence 8 - responsible for Signals Intelligence
MSS	Most Secret Source - the anonymous description of the RSS throughout WW2
NKVD	The Russian Secret Police - now the FSB
POW	Prisoner of War
RAF	Royal Air Force
RSGB	Radio Society of Great Britain
RSS	Radio Security Service
SCU	Special Communications Unit
SD	Sicherheitsdienst - intelligence agency of the German Nazi Party
SIS	Secret Intelligence Service
VI	Voluntary Interceptor
WI	Wireless Intercept - known as Y Stations
WT	Wireless Telegraphy

Harry Griffiths

Army, Royal Signals, Cpl

For service in support of the work of Bletchley Park during
World War Two

'We Also Served'

Although Morse code is no longer used by the military today,
it was used by the British military for decades, with a
skilled signaller able to send 30 words a minute.

The Royal British Legion has created this two petal remembrance poppy
which is detailed around the edges in Morse, reading:

WE WILL REMEMBER

In memory of Lt Cdr Bob Davidson AFC RN